CRAZY WOMAN HAS LEFT THE HOUSE - WILD WOMAN IS HOME

A Guide on How to Release

Crazy and Embrace Your

Wild Woman

Patricia C. Rockwood, MA
Transpersonal Psychology

Crazy Woman Has Left The House–WILD
WOMAN IS HOME

Dedication

This book is dedicated to all those who have suffered trauma at the hands of others yet choose to work toward their own healing. May this be part of your healing journey. And to those who offer healing and guidance for yourselves and to others, I salute you.

We ALL have the power to take charge of our own healing, whether done on our own or with help. Remember, you are not alone.

"What lies behind us and what lies before us are tiny matters compared to what lies within us".

- Ralph Waldo Emerson

Reader Bonus

For a free 10 minute introductory
consultation with Patricia
Email: **Wildspiritwave@gmail.com**
and put in the subject *Wild Woman Is Home*

Contents

Introduction

What began as my journey, the story of my life experience has changed in many ways—especially the beginning, where I describe my crazy woman behavior and reflections. Due to COVID-19 and what is happening globally, I have condensed my story, converting it into digestible words and (hopefully) relatable to anyone who reads them, including men and those who are marginalized.

We must maintain authority over our well-being and that of future generations. So how do we manage our lives and our bodies during this time? I offer ways that I have adopted from others and some of my own creative ideas. To heal trauma, both personally and as a species, we must also address the changes that need to happen, especially within ourselves, as it is now evident the rules and regulations of our current culture(s) are not sustainable.

I sincerely wish that this book helps those who have experienced trauma (part of the human condition) identify those triggers interfering with well-being and find their path to healing, connection, and self-care. Losing one's innocence, security, and the feeling of well-being leads to trauma and sometimes a loss of self-control. One can spend years (as I did) just trying to cope with daily life. Forging a way through the muck to the rich and beautiful place of contentment and deep happiness of self, despite what has been or is currently transpiring around you, is the goal.

I am profoundly humbled and grateful to have learned the grace and immensity of my being. I have learned ways to cope that have enriched my life, for my triggers are there to greet me. Now I understand them and have learned to welcome them as an opportunity to look. That piece of personal power brings me joy because it is an opportunity to change any behaviors I do not like about myself.

This guide will help you on your journey. I have learned to start from a place of well-being rather than woundedness. If you commit yourself to a similar passage, you will find more ease than you are currently experiencing.

I acquired a Master of Arts in Transformative Theories and Practices AKA Transformative Psychology from Atlantic University, Virginia Beach. I have always felt off, different, though people did not know this shadow side for the most part. Sound familiar? These feelings led me to search along a spiritual path. I pursued the above degree to learn to manage my anger and fears, embrace what I knew is my soul's beauty, and help others do the same.

After reading this book, you will walk away with a clear understanding of YOUR triggers and ways to cope, ways that you can continue to build upon as you heal. At the end of each chapter, you will find journal prompt questions. These are a suggestion, not a requirement, and are here to aid in your self-exploration. Your answers may evolve, and the insight you gain will grow as you learn to work with your inner crazy and wild woman. I invite you to receive these questions with curiosity.

It is time for a deeper understanding of why these scary, foreign feelings come up. Now is the time to reframe these feelings through coping skills rather than have them continue to keep you from moving toward a happier and more rewarding relationship with yourself.

The second half of the book offers practical spiritual information and advice with no dogma attached. You will have the opportunity to choose from rituals and ceremonies with the background knowledge provided from earlier chapters.

If not now, when? Step into full awareness and connection to your power, well-being, and happiness; this is your birthright. You are worthy and capable. I will show you how I have done it.

CHAPTER 1

Who Is Crazy Woman?

*T*his book was born on a morning when I began to release blame and guilt, both of myself and others. That moment, I acknowledged that I was 100% in charge of my own life and future, realizing that it was in my power to release these negative emotions. From the moment I sat writing, a gecko crawled on my foot, eating the mosquitoes feeding. I was in the universal flow. From that place of deep love and connection, I dedicate this book to all who share in what I call 'crazy' experiences and to those searching for a way forward into acting and living with consciousness, integrating our crazy, and embracing our inner wild.

In meditation and stillness, shortly after I released the above emotions, I was hurled into the heavens, where the concept for this book was born. My original thought was to create a workshop around my learning, but I was told, "It's too big for a workshop. It needs to reach too many!"

I want to clarify that this was not an *ah-ha* moment but rather a crazy, ugly birth. It was primordial and painful, done in isolation and sadness. Little by little, as the years went by, I became a bit crazier, a bit angrier, or perhaps I just became aware of the emotions hidden deep inside. These feelings continued to grow due to my unhappiness. My life wasn't going as planned: I didn't always make enough money, and I did not have a healthy work/life balance when I did. I felt that my experiences were not enriching enough. Mostly, I did not trust that my life would turn out okay, that I was going to be okay. So I focused my efforts on reframing, writing down the steps to help me move into a trust position. But how does one absorb that into the soul? The work was exhausting. The frustration was *crazy-making*. On top of this, I felt jealousy grow inside me towards those I loved and admired who were successful in ways that I wanted for myself. My dears, this is crazy-making thinking.

We have felt stuck in those thoughts allowing them to exist because we have abandoned ourselves in some respects. We choose our partners, close friends, families, even business responsibilities over taking care of our deepest needs. We may feel we have no choice due to an illness within the dynamics of the relationship, emotionally volatile connections, or even threatening behavior. We forget how to set boundaries, or worse yet, we never learned to develop them due to childhood circumstances. What is happening is that we have stopped showing up as ourselves! This lack of boundaries is where crazy woman thrives. My inner crazy woman manifested as temperamental and angry. The anger increased as time went on. I directed it at anyone or anything that would tolerate my negative behavior. What was happening? *I was shrinking!*

Many children are conditioned to ignore their physical and emotional needs, often from the moment of birth. Children, having minimal control over their bodies, are expected to stay quiet and still. Those raised as women receive an extra dose of indoctrination. They are taught gendered rules of behavior and manners, observing as boys are held to different standards and have more freedom. It is common for people to learn to suppress their needs and desires, playing small and quiet. Did you ever notice how assertive little boys get called leaders while powerful little girls get called bossy? These are the social norms that teach us to mask our authentic selves. This cultural coding results in a very ingrained practice of ignoring our bodies and our desires. I have worked with women who learned to refuse offers of snacks, food, and water to be polite and discreet. Others have held their urine and bowel movements for private locations, which often meant holding it until getting home.

Additionally, the gendered messaging on bodies and food is unavoidable; we learn early on to dislike our bodies and criticize ourselves for failing to meet an impossible standard of beauty. Many of us learn through developmental and social circumstances that deliver safety and acceptance through performing 'good behaviors' or acts of service and generally being compliant. By the time we are adults, we have been suppressing our body's natural communication methods for so long that we can no longer discern our authentic desires, only the ones we have learned that make us feel safe. Even our desires may be just a performance, as we seek out the materials and experiences we think we are supposed to, crafting a persona we believe would garner social approval.

I was so out of touch with my worth that I could not comfortably be present in my body. Anyone who has ever felt inclined towards people-pleasing and casual codependence may understand the stress you feel when a conflict breaks out in your family or friend group. Likely the discomfort is not our own, but instead that those we care about are upset, and the easiest way to feel comfortable again is finding a quick resolution. There were decades I performed this role with a former partner. I thought it was expected of me to keep the peace. We become masters at *fixing*, at making people happy by giving them what they want. This social script has become so ingrained in our society that it's almost rude not to follow someone who storms off upset. We may give a lover the cold shoulder and resent them for not interpreting that non-communication as an invitation to repair.

All this fixing was exhausting, and sometimes I did not have the kind of energy it required. I would reach the limits of my emotional tolerance, then boom! My *fight* impulse would manifest. If I felt forced into self-betrayal, an ugly part of me would get triggered—my inner crazy woman. Her rage consumed me, coming out of me in tantrums and meltdowns. I was relatively easy-going—until I wasn't! *Is this me?* I asked myself. I was embarrassed at this side of myself, this person who seemed to come out without warning. My friends and family accepted these outbursts from me. Men from my past would say, "you used to get so mad." I admit I feel mortified as I describe this and have sat with myself in sadness for the woman who felt so trapped that she 'snapped.' I felt like a nasty, crazy bitch! Sometimes we must be *who-we-are-not* to become *who-we-truly-are*, but I decided she couldn't possibly be me and distanced myself from this crazy woman. I made strenuous efforts to control myself, attempting to model a socially acceptable, soft, timid woman who didn't get angry or bothered. I suppressed behaviors, reactions, emotions, and yet she still showed up uninvited— I had to explore why!

Crazy woman is an archetypal figure who exists in the collective unconscious. She represents the shadow side of our wise woman in the forest; the label 'crazy' comes from the rumors and stories that get spread about her. Crazy woman arises when we do not or cannot honor our inner wise woman. Crazy woman comes out when we have had *enough*. What happens in the stories when people do not heed the wisdom of the inner wise woman? It often does not turn out well for those protagonists. Dr. Clarissa Pinkola Estes introduces the archetype of *feral woman* in her bestseller, *Women Who Run with the Wolves*.[1] Feral woman was once "in her rightful wild mind." However, due to events or experiences, she adopts an untamed state—one without a solid connection to the instincts that kept her alive and safe. Our crazy woman is one of the many faces of feral women.

Life trauma has morphed her instincts to the degree that she overreacts, underreacts, freezes, panics. How many of us have felt emotions well up in our bodies and willfully shoved them down to maintain outward appearances and defer to the comfort of others? We make room for crazy woman to arise when we do not make space for the authentic spectrum of emotion we feel at any given moment. Ultimately, crazy woman comes out when *she* decides, not when we let her. She comes out sideways, spewing resentment at our closest allies. Her mind is filled with paranoia and unease, lashing out with our worst temper or even infiltrating our bodies, where she can render our muscles useless with somatic pain for days.

There are so many different versions of this story. When feelings have nowhere to go, emotional pressure builds and explodes through the cracks in our defenses. This (often unconscious) manifestation of negative emotion is a function of the shadow self, a collection of triggers and traits that the ideal self (the ego) would like to keep at a distance. These are the personality traits that we disown out of shame. Crazy woman is an archetypal representation of these feminine shadows. We carry these shadows within us, magnified by the pressures of our modern collective consciousness.

'Crazy' is one of the most common labels placed on a threatening woman to put her in her place and remind her of her lesser status in the world. Some of us have been labeled crazy by others (or even ourselves), using it to dismiss or invalidate our thoughts, feelings, and desires. Throughout history, women in "civilized" societies have been discredited and disempowered by being labeled crazy, emotional, or hysterical. The stigma of crazy may have led you to suppress your truth. How many of us have squashed our feelings down to remain small and unobtrusive? We distance ourselves from our flaws and challenges, blinding ourselves to real wounds that need our love and attention. By taking ownership of the label crazy, we begin to shift the power structures behind it. So, it's okay if you don't identify with the word crazy. If there is another word, you resonate with, feel free to use that for yourself. In this narrative, crazy is a stand-in for many other emotions "well-behaved" women should not express.

I want to take a moment to reflect on some things happening in the world today. The patriarchy of our society has also profoundly affected men. My editor, Viviana, wisely pointed out that the masculine is also people who identify with and as the masculine. For those who have found their authentic selves as transgender or non-binary, we honor their variance. I think in binary terms because that is how I have been socialized to relate. But I am learning to connect and embrace more openly because it is essential to acknowledge how this socialization has traditionally excluded sacred variance. I hope to be inclusive to all free thinkers and fringe dwellers (such as myself) because we are whole human beings, no matter how we identify. When referring to the Sacred Feminine and Sacred Masculine, I refer to the core traits of energies we all carry within ourselves, regardless of gender identity.

The dominant culture of our society has taught us to fear the wild woman, who has been historically marginalized by mainstream society. The ideological teaching has been that wild women are evil or feral. Feral beings are creatures to be managed, deemed untamable. The sleeping masculine, still rooted in the patriarchy, fears the untamable feminine power, believing his failure to dominate the feral will strip him of masculinity. When a wild woman is typecast as an evil sorceress, the comfortable alternative is to hide in the protection of vilifying her as a crazy woman. In reality, a true wild woman is AWAKE and has so much more to give than her righteous anger. To cultivate our own space and wholeness for expansion is why the journey from crazy to wild is critical. It is not just a journey of self-healing; it is a journey of planetary healing, one that must be inclusive of the wounded masculine as well.

I remember hearing an interview with Desmond Tutu, where he says, "As long as there are conditions in many parts of the world that make people desperate: poverty, disease, ignorance, etc., you cannot 'win a war against terror.' I hope that we will discover soon that we can survive, only together. We can prosper only together. People are beginning to realize you can't have pockets of prosperity in one part of the world, and huge deserts of poverty and deprivation in another, believing you can have a stable, secure world."[2]

We cannot ignore the areas where growth is still needed, even as other areas prosper. In many ways, these substandard conditions in the world are crazy-making. We know folks cannot move towards self-actualization when they are concerned about basic needs such as safety, food, and shelter. In many ways, societal systems suffer from a sickness—namely inequality and greed—that creates ongoing power imbalances.

Crazy is not wholly wrong, dark, or negative; life is not so simple that we can boil it down to black/white dichotomies of good/evil or crazy/sane. The spectrum of human emotions and experiences is much more nuanced than that. Our feelings are traffic signs, leading us to deeper wounds and unconscious influences. Feelings are not dictated by conscious thought and intention. They arise within us from an unconscious place where they live. Many of us are taught through society to judge our feelings. As children, it starts as simple as happy = good, sad or mad = bad. Part of engaging in this process involves paying attention to the judgments we issue ourselves. Invite yourself to practice holding space for every emotion that wells up inside you because they are *all* valid. You do not need to know where they come from or why they arose in the first place, just that they are yours.

When we begin the practice of increasing our emotional intelligence, of learning to sense our bodies' internal state(s) through introspection, it can be challenging to discern all the shades of gray that fall between the extremes on the emotional spectrum. For some of us, the most challenging and sometimes unavoidable emotion can be rage. When we have never been taught how to hold anger, we become vulnerable and uncontrollable. Many of us have survived by holding our truths inside. We did not allow ourselves to feel or express anger, knowing we would be punished for expressing such feelings.

So when you start doing the work of understanding the scale of what you have endured, you realize that you were not protected and kept safe as you should have been. The latent part of you recognizes that you have been harmed by more than just your abuser, that you have also been harmed by the family that allowed this and the society that created this. Then you become enraged. This rage is not destructive—it is not aggression or violence. It is an expression of violated boundaries and of what you will no longer tolerate.

Think about your childhood. Did you over-or under-express anger? In therapy, I was directed to express the rage inside me, which was very uncomfortable! After all, I had worked hard to no longer express it and was even successful suppressing it for a time. My therapist encouraged me to try hitting pillows or consciously shouting to move energy. I did not enjoy or appreciate it because of exactly what I explained above: I had never been taught to hold space for my anger though I was furious. I did not know how to appreciate what it was trying to say. However, in hindsight, I was given a tool to release rage appropriately, which I have used only a time or two in private.

Holding space for rage can either be very frightening or very liberating. Most important is asking *why* the rage and noticing that it can sometimes be compounded with other emotions. For example, many have learned other coping mechanisms: overeating, and daydreaming (dissociating) to protect themselves via the few tools that allow us to feel good. This is especially true when we are young and have few resources for emotional support. Sometimes rage can feel easier to hold than fear. This makes sense as anger can feel powerful while fear can feel like weakness. Notice that your first impulse when identifying your anger may be to dismiss the rage or call it out as a function of the ego. I invite you to greet your fury, let it know that it is welcome and safe here, that you are willing to listen. It is natural and valid. I encourage you to practice journaling *why* and *what* you are angry about with self-awareness and honesty.

We choose to approach all our shadow work with the archetype of crazy woman because of how earnestly we would like *not* to be her, knowing the only way out is to work through the memories and corresponding emotions.

Our quest is to understand our crazy woman better. We want to honor her and the shadow work she represents and integrate her wisdom with the ideal self. As we become deeply acquainted with her, she leads us on a journey to find the wild woman inside us all.

Journal Questions

1. Who is your crazy woman? Meaning, how does she show up?
2. Do you know where she comes from?
3. Do you know why she is here?

CHAPTER 2

The Trauma Journey

Y ou are, right at this moment, on a precipice. Trust that you will catch yourself if you step off. Embrace the love of yourself and go for it. I promise you will not regret it. Well, you might at first. There will be twinges of *was that the right call?* There will be moments of wanting to please those who are afraid of your growth. Will things fall away that you care about? Most likely. People too? Probably. Still, the freedom of self-love calls inviting creativity and joyful expression to flow through your body. And a vitality fills you after you start to uncover the authentic self. For it becomes a part of you, it grows as you claw your way up and out of sadness, loneliness, and the grief of letting go, releasing fear, which is often an illusion of perception. This is part of the wild work, improvising and foraging our way to wholeness. And it is big work. This big work leads to more and more precipices, more and more jumps into opportunities for embodiment and wisdom. Learning to feel and discern our embodied, *yes* and *no,* is crucial to know what we need and truly desire.

Sometimes when we hear the word *desire,* it sounds like a luxury. A want versus a need. There are schools of Buddhism that believe suffering is caused by desire and enlightenment is gained through detachment.[3] Those of us exposed to Judeo-Christian theology may have inferred growing up that coveting is bad, especially when coveting something belonging to others or a certain forbidden apple. For years I refused to listen to my deeper urges, my true feelings because I wanted to make my life function well, the way it was *supposed to.* Only it wasn't working—I FELT CRAZY! For so long, I was afraid of being crazy, of being dismissed for mental illness. Still, I understand now that my fear, avoidance, and denial of crazy created ideal conditions for crazy-making thinking to abound. I felt shame when I could not be happy for friends who were in touch with their desires, thinking *why they get to have these gifts, but not me?*

Working with our desires involves truly discerning between what is yours and what is not. *Who is this in service of? Who does this belong to? Where do I start and the people I am in relationship with end?* The answer is not always cut and dry, sometimes it's a blended answer, and the romanticization of selflessness and codependent love certainly muddles the options. Yes, we must care for each other as a collective, but we must also take responsibility for that which is ours and offer others the opportunity to manage their own emotions and experiences. I continued to observe myself and my desire to please, sitting in conversation with this desire, dancing with the discomfort of observing tension and waiting instead of fixing or fighting, so again I asked myself, *does this serve me beyond resolving a point of relational tension or the stress of others' discomfort?* The answer was unclear for a long time, but slowly a quiet, whispering *No* began to form.

I consciously noticed my desire to please and the risk of self-betrayal—sometimes choosing it anyway! The inner conflict to resolve tension was greater than the desire for my own truth—perhaps because I did not yet have a taste for it, or I forgot and lost the taste. When you have not truly tasted this wildness inside yourself before, it can feel too strange to swallow. So I spent another couple of years watching myself choose self-betrayal and self-shaming for not having the strength to resist the muscle memory of people-pleasing.

Have you noticed that anytime we try to make personal changes, we risk ending in a shame cycle? This is why diets are a multi-billion dollar industry because they know they can exploit this shame. Shame is our internalized sense of distress that shows up when we perceive that we have done something wrong, either by personal or societal standards. Do you remember how you felt when you said the wrong answer in front of your whole class? I can feel the heat in my cheeks just thinking about some of my embarrassing memories; it is such a visceral emotion. If it weren't so tied to our bodies, I imagine shame would have much less power than it does. Instead, it makes us want to leave our bodies when we are overwhelmed by it. That is one of the ways I determine whether I might be feeling some shame or fear. If I feel inclined to dissociate, whether through mindless hours on social media or Netflix or a strong craving for a couple of adult beverages, that is an invitation to look deeper into my body. Once I could discern how shame feels inside me and where it lives, I could practice tolerating it and just being with it.

But before I had learned to work with this shame, it had me back in crazy woman thinking! I found if I judged myself negatively, blaming and shaming myself for my nervous system's best attempt to find safety, I was leaving the door right open for crazy woman to take over, and she had a laundry list of bones to pick. So I dedicated myself to my inner spiritual work, trying to manifest my wise woman self. I knew she was there somewhere; I had encountered her before in peak experiences and altered states. My spiritual experiences helped me harness insight and deepened my discernment, but try as I might, I could not meditate or journey this ire away.

As I became aware of the ways I avoided being present, what I saw scared me. By the time I was in my late twenties, I was drinking more alcohol than I would care to admit and partying dangerously. I was in denial about the dark truths inside of me that I was trying to suppress through sensation seeking. I knew if I did not stop soon, I would lose myself completely. Self-love felt far away for me, but I met a man who was charming and charismatic. He felt solid and grounded, and there was a deep love between us. I thought deep love was losing yourself in someone else;

after all, that seems to be how most of the love stories go in the movies. As the years went by, I put my ambitions and desires aside, investing in my husband and marriage.

Over time I became more attracted to alternative spirituality and shamanism. I had memories of practicing it as a child in making and playing my own drum after a traumatic episode. How I knew to do that, I do not know. I only know it worked for me, so when the opportunities for more learning came my way, I wanted to explore these gifts and grow a practice helping others. This led to attaining my graduate degree in transformational psychology.

However, the marriage became threatened. There was tension between the desires that were awakening inside of me and my role in my marriage. As I asserted myself and my desires and worked to unlearn the self-imposed shame, this caused an even deeper rupture in my marriage. When we are driven towards our own personal evolution, sometimes the people around us do not know how to support us in the ways that we need. This leads to deep conflict within ourselves between the self and the other.

As this conflict built within me and my relationships, decades of pent-up emotions started surfacing, alienating strangers and loved ones alike. There were days, months, and even years when there was ambivalence. *Where is my life going? How am I going to create what I am trying to create? What are my truest passions?* I flailed around with these questions, dealing with resistance both within myself and from others. Trying to free myself from the constraints of feeling unloved, searching for myself through spiritual discipline, and trying to zero in on my dream, I would touch it, only to think in my private thoughts. *No, that can't possibly be for me.* Despite the challenges, I continued to reach for my purpose, searching and being grateful most of all for the wild woman in me who never gave up on herself.

Now people who know me know that I am an empathetic person, that I love with loyalty. But this split I felt between my ego and my higher consciousness was driving me crazy. So what did I do? I left my husband; I left my home, I sold my business. I moved across two oceans and a continent. And guess what happened? Crazy woman came right along with me, unleashing herself in ways I would never have expected. I was in the belly of the beast, scared to death because I thought I was losing my mind! It felt like I had no support system; I did not know anyone in this strange place I had landed. I left my comfort zone and catapulted myself into staring these ugly, crazy aspects of myself in the face. Let me tell you, it sucked! It is not fun or pretty or even liberating when you're struggling to keep fighting that beast.

As I came out on the other side of this exhausting dance with crazy woman, I knew it was my journey to share this experience with others so that they may work with crazy and wild and find the truth inside themselves. So I sat down to write my story; when it was done, I sent it off to Viviana Scarlet, my editor and a longtime friend whom I met when she was 11 years old; throughout the decades, we have come together to share various practical and esoteric arts. I taught her how to ride horses and work with a variety of animals—this was always a gift I was known for. When she became a teenager, she expressed interest in shamanism while studying the shamanic arts and apprenticing with a shaman. I invited her to help me practice my learning in one-on-one work with me and some of my workshops. We both pursued different forms of higher education and came together again to edit my master's thesis on Constellation Work and the Medicine Wheel in 2010. That same summer, I taught her everything I knew about astrology.

When I needed an editor for this manuscript that poured out of my soul after my dance with crazy woman, Viviana was a natural choice. I originally expected my audience to be limited to women over 50 who related to my experiences of putting other people (notably the patriarchy) before ourselves. When Viviana became immersed in my manuscript and heard the message in a way that made sense to her, it occurred to us that we could reach more people than I had realized. She explained to me that "younger generations related to this work too, and had also been enduring the trauma of capitalism, misogyny, racism and heteronormativity, as well as innumerable other y's and isms."

We both noticed shifts in consciousness occurring in our respective communities— people choosing to go on wellness retreats instead of a resort vacation, people vowing to resolve their trauma not to pass it on, myriad conversations on boundaries and removing toxic people in their lives, old friends and loved ones experiencing spiritual awakenings and joining our collective conscious revolution for a better planet and safer communities.

I felt safer sharing my spiritual interests and claiming them as the gifts they are: healing tools. I found more and more people resonating with my words, and I realized it is all too common an experience to lose oneself to and in one's trauma. It was clear that what I knew as crazy was really just the face of trauma that I (along with countless others) was used to wearing.

Journal Questions

1. How do you avoid being present?
2. What is a deep-down soul desire that you hold but have not ventured into?
3. What has been your crazy and wild dance? How does the above question relate to this question?

CHAPTER 3

Does Crazy Come From Fear? A Look At Trauma

What if I don't have trauma? You might be asking yourself. Chances are, you have experienced things in this lifetime that left a mark on your spirit. It is understood that these wounds can vary in size and scope; psychologists agree that they may have a cumulative effect. And it is okay if you do not identify with your trauma; it can feel safer to be distant from our pain. It is important to note, however, that some of this dis-ownership of pain is a result of our social programming and how we are taught to compare ourselves to others. Our needs become invalidated by the greater needs of others when, in actuality, we are all entitled to our various needs, especially our emotional needs, and they have very little to do with the experiences of others.

As we continue to develop our understanding of our own traumas and the dynamics that prevent us from showing up as ourselves, we can use that awareness to harness our fears to take small steps toward looking at our wounds. Do not hide from your fear or your wounds. One of the comments I received as feedback when sharing early drafts of this book was, "Well, I don't know about crazy coming from fear. But that trauma stuff, I sure see that!" How interesting that people could access the trauma but quickly distance themselves from crazy and fear. We rarely willingly identify as afraid or terrified—this is an unflattering vulnerability. Society tells children, "Don't be afraid" instead of "It's okay to be afraid." Schoolyard bullies throw around epithets such as "scaredy-cat." We wear strength and bravery as armor when authentic vulnerability may offer us the protection we seek. This is running rampant in our society, even more so today. Why are we so afraid of fear? It cannot be released until it is felt and identified.

Clinically, trauma is largely characterized as an event or experience that triggers the body's stress hormones and defense mechanisms. We all have a different standard for what that intangible, bad thing might be, so we continually tell ourselves that what happened to us wasn't as bad as what happened to the other guy, so it's not a big deal. It's a common response to minimize the event. How is that working for you? It may not serve you, but know that the minimization of trauma is, in fact, a standard response to trauma. Our instinct is to swallow the pain, especially before we've developed our trauma skills when we're unsure of how to integrate the experience. In its infinite wisdom, the body helps us manage what the psyche cannot, hiding away the scars of trauma in the very fibers of our being. In addition to what we experience in this lifetime, the study of epigenetics has confirmed that we transmit genetic mutations to future generations. Traumatic stress has been proven to influence these epigenetic changes. The trauma stored in our bodies is a combination of our lived experiences and our inherited experiences.

Our DNA carries the wounds of our ancestors' experiences. Just as their experiences shape us, our experiences and conscious reflection can heal these evolutionary scars. Our ancestors' DNA, from an energetic perspective, connects us primarily to the first two energy centers of our biological family and our ancestors. It makes total sense; after all, every living thing possesses DNA, which is why I have extended this work into nature as well. Our root center grounds us to the earth.

Our bodies are regulated by a nervous system that is both electrical and hormonal. It is the energetic highway that connects each piece of your body together like an intricate machine. Many indigenous cultures throughout the world have long asserted that we carry our ancestors inside of us. Epigenetics is the science of how. These cultures also had intimate knowledge of the body and working with the nervous system, such as connecting with energy centers in the body, which you may be familiar with as *chakras*. Dr. Carl Jung explored the chakras and illustrated their Hindu meanings with Biblical examples, such as Catholic fascination with Mary's sacred heart. He described how other cultures had located consciousness within different areas of the body other than the head, locating the self in the heart or diaphragm. He found that chakra work can even inspire deep spiritual experiences that can influence psychological healing. It makes sense, then, that these energy centers actually correspond with your corporeal neural network, where tangles of nerves cross over each other, exchanging information. This is where those energy centers are, strung together by our vagus nerve, the longest nerve in our body that runs the length of our spine. Somatic expert Resmaa Menakem aptly calls it the 'soul nerve.' I will talk more about this in Chapter 6.

There are a variety of ways the nervous system attempts to cope with lived and inherited traumatic stress. Our autonomic nervous system is responsible for our biological fear defenses, which kick in whenever the body perceives danger and may set a bodily fear response in the wake of serious trauma.

Fight or Flight

Many of us are familiar with our arousal responses from the sympathetic nervous system: the fight-or-flight response releases a flood of stress hormones and adrenaline to mitigate perceived danger by preparing you to protect yourself. This emergency response puts the body on a sort of autopilot for managing a crisis—heart rate increases, blood rushes to various parts of your body, breath quickens, etc. This bodily response may or may not be appropriate based on the stimuli, but the lived and inherited traumas imprint triggers in the body so that when (perceivably) similar circumstances recur, the body sends out a strong instinctual response to guard against potential danger.

Freeze or Fawn

The other part of the autonomic nervous system, the parasympathetic nervous system, is responsible for the freeze-or-faint response. Sometimes the body's response to trauma is hypoarousal, halting bodily responses and at times resulting in out-of-body dissociative experiences. Freeze responses often lead to deep self-blame, as we wonder, *Why didn't I fight back?* Or *Why didn't I scream?* Self-blame is a nearly ubiquitous survivor response, a natural attempt to make sense of something by assigning control to the various players. Since we can exert the most control on ourselves, we tend to start there. The psyche can have a hard time processing trauma, so gaps in memory are common, especially following a dissociative episode. It is possible that our freeze response keeps us safe in a dangerous scenario. Loss of consciousness can happen in extreme circumstances if the vasovagal nerve overreacts to emotional stimuli, resulting in a faint response.

I was also introduced to another trauma response many are unfamiliar with that is starting to gain some attention, the "fawn" response. This is still a parasympathetic nervous system response; the ventral vagal cortex is responsible for this more socially focused trauma response. A fawn response comes from a learned need to soothe one's abuser and ensure safety through compliance and pleasing.

I recall books on codependency and people-pleasing being a large subset of the self-help genre in the 80s and 90s. These are the fawn responses by an older name. Fawning is notably common among survivors of developmental childhood neglect and abuse. Fawners have trouble taking up space, experiencing pleasure, having their own needs met. They learn to place others above themselves as a survival strategy. Now that this trauma response is becoming better understood and identified, we see a lot of discussion on social media and various trauma blogs. Women tend to be socialized to stay small and serve others; it is no wonder many of us resonate so much with the fawn trauma response.

Trauma expert Pete Walker theorizes that most of us have a predominant response type based on how we have adapted to trauma and stress. Your dominant trauma response may still come up each time you are triggered. This brings up the many faces of crazy, which are so easy for us to identify. It is clear that the body, mainly the nervous system, holds on to these early imprints of trauma and continues to employ these survival instincts throughout the lifetime. When we become trauma-informed, we approach our coping mechanisms and trauma responses with empathy and compassion, understanding that these are autonomic or unconscious responses. Unpacking our trauma and re-setting our nervous system's responses involves conscious effort to work the mind, spirit, *and* body. The trauma literature to date supports that healing trauma cannot be done by talk therapy alone: we also need a somatic approach to "move our issues through our tissues" (a quote learned during my yoga teacher training). A movement practice is integral to a whole mind-body-spirit approach. For many, it may be the missing ingredient.

These predominant responses can have long-term effects that come up later in ways that we would benefit from exploring. Sometimes we feel our body reacting to situations in a way we do not understand. It may feel like an overreaction, or a mismatched response, which is an indication that underlying trauma is either hidden from our consciousness or is part of our inherited instincts.

When I find myself feeling more triggered than seems reasonable, I realize that it is coming from a place I cannot access. In the past, this may have been frustrating because I felt shame about my overreaction. I know now that these hidden traumas are out of reach for my consciousness because they are coming from my ancestral DNA or traumas that caused me to dissociate entirely from my body.

This is also why understanding our racial and ethnic identities and doing the work to dismantle systems of oppression are so important. Marginalized bodies are carrying the wounds of their oppressed ancestors and are at higher risk for traumatic symptoms. When we heal ourselves, we heal our lineage.

Because trauma is a form of stress, it is deeply intertwined with fear. When our minds and bodies do not yet have a framework for understanding fear, we are more likely to escape our bodies entirely. This may lead to a freeze response, in which the stress causes brain pathways to shut down. For me, this led to a lot of gaps in my memory and interfered with my ability to learn. My family dismissed this and thought I just wasn't very smart. As I learned to cope with this challenge, I came to understand that my learning difficulties were related to my trauma history. As a trauma survivor, I always felt behind. I had to struggle to keep up.

As I was going through my teenage years, I met "normal" people and started hanging out with them. I watched how they learned and figured out for myself how to adapt my own learning. I did this without any understanding of what I was doing; I just knew I wanted to be normal. I got good enough at *faking* normal, like when I wrote messily on my tests in the hopes that my teacher would see enough of the right answers to pass me, compensating enough to graduate. Stress puts us at a disadvantage because our brains are focused on survival rather than on thriving. If this resonates with you, understand that this is a lifelong challenge. You will watch others who are seemingly able to function better achieve at a level you will most likely not be able to attain. Your skills and efforts are valid—make peace with them. Honor who you are. And explore the gifts you do carry.

I remember sitting at the dining table in my mother's home while my brother was visiting. The three of us were talking when I said something that made my brother raise his eyebrows and look at my mother. I will never forget the moment when I heard her say, "Oh yes, she is quite smart. I think she is smarter than I am." Finally, some validation. But by then, I was 19 years old, and I had already internalized that I wasn't good enough, something that I still struggle with. Do you see the domino effect?

It was not until my late 30's when I was completing my undergraduate degree that I was diagnosed with a learning disability. I did not understand what was going on in my classes. Fortunately, I had a Spanish teacher who saw that I was capable of A-level conversational Spanish but could not write down what was in my head. I felt so stupid when she sent me to the disabilities department, where I was interviewed by a blind woman. *Now there is a REAL disability*, I said to myself. She referred me to a specialist who then sent me to get my IQ tested. My results were typical, but my reading and writing processing skills were significantly inhibited, including math, where the numbers seemed to have a mind of their own. A psychologist I worked with said that my learning disability likely came from the severe stress of ongoing childhood trauma.

The good news is, with this knowledge and understanding, I began self-healing work on my mental and emotional body by incorporating spiritual and physical practices. Many of my neural pathways have been regrown, and I have discovered that I am incredibly capable. Even so, I still struggle and will until my dying day. Many things simply feel overwhelming in my daily life.

Though I have a documented learning disability, I still do everything in my power to hide it. Why? It is my deepest, darkest shadow. I simply do not feel good enough; it is embarrassing. Though I have worked very hard on sharpening and keeping my brain supple, some pathways simply are not there, and that is okay. It is not my fault, but it is in my power to be compassionate with myself about my shadows.

Once we accept that it was not our fault, we must go deeper. The more difficult work remains because these shadow parts of our personalities are not easy to take ownership of. We may not understand what is going on, but rather, we are triggered into a physiological response, such as anger. It is only by digging deeply into these parts of ourselves we would like to distance ourselves from that we can understand and learn to deal with these triggers. This does not mean the feelings no longer arise, but rather we learn techniques to deal with them when they do. We practice breathing into the parts of ourselves that bring up shame. Understanding your shadows is crucial; you may find that they are hiding just below the surface. One morning Viviana and I were in a coffee shop working when she suggested I talk about the above shadow in this book. I burst into tears because of how viscerally I could feel the fear rising in my body. Her simple suggestion caused a reaction in me so volatile that I had to step outside to collect myself. Having such strong instant reactions makes us feel (and can even lead others to perceive us as) CRAZY.

Journal Questions

1. How are you invalidating yourself due to fear of your shadows?
2. Do you have any memories that elicit strong visceral reactions? Have you ever found yourself minimizing these reactions or events in your life?

CHAPTER 4

How to Get in Touch With Crazy Woman and the Soul Woundings Where Our Triggers Originate

One does not become enlightened by imagining figures of light, but by making the darkness conscious. The latter procedure, however, is disagreeable and therefore not popular.'–C. G. Jung

We spend too much time denying our crazy. Crazy is just a form of fear. Part of the wild woman process is to face fear and release it into self-love. This includes the fear (the lie) that we are not good enough. We can shepherd ourselves from the subjective self to the ideal goal-self, recognizing that crazy woman is crazy because of life experiences. Crazy woman has helped you to survive, she had a purpose, and she was good at her work. If you look, you will find the anger and pain she carries kept you alive in some way. So yes, we thank crazy woman and invite her to leave, assuring her that we will protect ourselves and our vulnerable parts. While we are releasing her, we may feel inclined to forgive her. We forgive all the unintentional hurt she caused, the moments where we may have felt far away from ourselves, the crazy experiences that we reflect on with shame. And we even forgive the intentional, too, the fight instincts that moved you through triggers and defenses. Eckhart Tolle, in *A New Earth,* said, "To recognize one's own insanity is, of course, the arising of sanity, the beginning of healing and transcendence."[4]

We forgive the negative aspects of the self that she has carried and continue to thank her. Because, babe, she brought us to this place of huge evolutionary growth. She brought you and me to this place where we can recognize our own insanity. This is the place where the wild woman resides, in what Brené Brown calls "the wilderness." The question is, *how* do we encourage crazy to leave the house? *How* do we keep her from eating us alive until our precious hearts feel like dried-up prune pits? We must move through this because if we do not, we will remain attached to suffering, and crazy women may never leave, and then we may not find our wild hearts.

So, let's reflect on how to help crazy leave the house. You do not need to go to the extremes I did, like leaving everything behind, moving halfway across the world, and starting from scratch. Or maybe you do—only you can discover your path. I know that by doing what I did, I created a safe place for myself to explore and discover pieces of myself and remember parts of myself that I might have lost along the way. It was a challenging move and one that came with its own loneliness and sadness. There was something to be gained on the other side, but taking that leap involved some painful loss. When I removed some of the *noise* that was in my life prior to making this big move, I realized that I have been searching for a sense of belonging for many years, hoping to find my soul community of like-minded thinkers and creators. Many of our wounds occur in a relational context—it makes sense that some of our healing must also be found in that relational space. The paradox here is that we need to work both on an individual level towards wholeness of self and on a relational level for the purpose of practicing and living authentic intimacy with our soul friends. The choices we make and have made have a lasting impact.

In the individual sphere, for your internal work, you can create a self-imposed spiritual retreat as did I, spending several months alone at a friends' home while she was away. I focused on the tools of transformation that were at my disposal, primarily shamanism, a practice I had been drawn to intuitively and instinctually since I was five years old. It has always immediately connected me to "wild woman." Shamanism taught me to embrace my wild woman in all her entirety.

I cannot fully express in words the deep soul meditative experiences shamanic journeying has provided me over the years; I can only hope to share pieces of it through this book and my personal shamanic offerings.

Shamanism can lead one on their own path of co-creation with the universe. So many of us wild women are envisioning a time when this and other similar types of exploration were and will again be a part of our collective common experiences every day. I truly believe that by embracing this path, we can renew ourselves and the earth. Shamanism is an ancient practice that embraces all that is, as a whole; it is universal. There are those who advocate that we might call it "animism," which describes one of the central tenets of shamanism: that each and every thing, big or small, sentient being or not, from the animals to geological features, has a spirit and energy. As we delve into this way of seeing the world, we begin to feel the interconnectedness of all things. And as we each heal ourselves, we also heal the collective, building on the sacred evolution of spirit. I feel it is the most direct path not only for working with wild women but for connecting with an authentic sacred masculine too. To heal the planet, we must embrace ways that empower both the feminine and the masculine, going directly into our soul wounds and the wounds of the planet. It is in this way that the feminine can hold the vision while the masculine rebuilds, thus repairing ourselves and our future using tools that reclaim and decolonize. It does not matter if you identify as a man or a woman; as Viv says, "souls do not have a gender." What matters is that we utilize the gift of this era, being on the edge of new conscious frontiers, where we can innovatively incorporate ancient knowledge with new technologies.

I want to look at the original ways, for they are still with us. There are those who have ensured this knowledge has not died out, sacred keepers of tradition and mystery. One of the deepest wounds of the patriarchy has been the indoctrination and subjugation of the sacred masculine, which was then exploited to oppress the feminine. We know the feminine has suffered; wild woman has been controlled and groomed. This may be our original soul wound, early experiences that teach us to betray our bodies and our intuition. As we have discussions around these experiences, we wild women can feel this consciousness blowing up. For us, the healing is coming through the belly of the mother; it rises up through our being.

But what about the sacred masculine? The man must relearn to receive from wild women as well, to work with nature in its original form, as we were meant to. These paths teach us how to feel, confront, and transmute fear, allowing us to go where our souls call us. Women historically have maintained social networks where we may instinctively be practicing collaborative wisdom. I am reminded of Red Tents, moontime rituals, and the ability of menopausal women to gather on sleepless nights with the knowledge that they can rest during the day. Now we are expected to power through the above fatigues. These ways of honoring the natural rhythms have been lost in mainstream western culture, but women are still encouraged and expected to work in groups.

The domesticated masculine is expected to be ruggedly independent and autonomous. He must be strong and capable of surviving without much help. He must be the provider, protector, savior. And that can be terrifying because the blueprint for collaborative, loving masculinity has been erased. This has forced the masculine to have no choice but to embody the roles forced upon them, even to the point where they are not allowed to express the pain and fear they carry in their bodies. Boys who have lost a father figure are told to step up and be the man, protect their mother and siblings. *What?* That is a lot of pressure to put on a grown man, much less a child. Yet here we are, in a culture that has unrealistic, idealistic expectations of men. We spend so much of our lives thinking about how opposite the masculine and feminine are and how different those who embody these qualities are. You might remember a popular book from the 90s about how we are from different planets! It can feel that way sometimes, sure. Still, if we really boil down the tension and remove the labels, genders, and presumptions, we are left with the same feeling of emptiness, purposelessness, and failure, as we insist on fitting ourselves into the roles imposed upon us. All the while, an ancient wildness inside wonders, *is this it?* I have known men who have experienced tremendous soul wounds and have never been given the space to be wounded. We may have grown up thinking boys don't cry, nor should they, yet men carry this invisible burden that requires them to be strong while at the same time not allowing them the power to right wrongs and sometimes even to speak! This, too, is a wounding of colonization.

We, as women, know how trauma feels in our bodies. We are allowed to express our pain, even expected to be emotional and dramatic sometimes. I knew a beautiful man who had to undergo complete blood transfusions about once a month just to stay alive. I watched him power through, then return to work because he had no choice. One day he and I were having a conversation about pain. I asked him, "Where is it in your body?" That he could describe. Then I asked him what he does with it; he had no idea what I meant. I explained that our society teaches men that they must power through their pain, ignore it. I suggested instead that he focus on the pain, giving it love and attention. He was shocked at the concept, Christian Fundamentalist that he was. But you know, he loved the idea. He practiced this mini shamanic healing upon himself instinctively through a simple suggestion. I, as the feminine, knew he could harness the information he needed to perform self-healing without my help, as he carried this ancient wisdom in his DNA.

If we look at this in the old way, we see where the feminine is the vessel, the holy grail, and the masculine is the tool. While the vessel holds space for the wisdom to sit, it is the masculine who holds the opposite of space: matter. Man is matter and form. The wild woman archetype embodies the foreseers, the front runners, the space holders. The sacred masculine archetype must continue to do their own circles—they are creators. We need them in our feminine energy circles because they are our complementary anchors. And so many, so very many hold the knowledge that we need.

Unity and flexibility are the only way forward. The Awakened Masculine practices vulnerability and intuition if he is given the space to do so. Ask a man about his emotions, and he might feel unsafe. Ask him about the pain he feels in his body, and he can talk about it. Give him a suggestion, and he may intuitively know how to heal himself. And then he will know how to heal humanity and the planet as well.

A wild woman may feel spider woman working through her as we weave the fabric of humanity together. The sacred masculine can also create healing and receive and offer protection. It is as simple as connecting through the five elements. Feel into this: it is right. It is the way forward. It is so because we are no longer acting against our core values. Our core values are not what colonialism and patriarchy have us practicing: greed, capitalism, over-productivity, looting of finite natural resources, erasure of the old ways. Most humans really do love and respect the natural environment and each other.

Exploring shamanic traditions was my path, and, as I mentioned, my first self healing experience was as a child of four or five. After a traumatic event, I remember going into the kitchen and picking up an empty coffee can. I got paper and crayons, glue and a new unsharpened pencil. I drew Native North Americans on horseback with teepees and nature. I glued the artwork onto the can; this was all pre-kindergarten in the mid-1960s. How I knew to do this, heal myself from the pain of the abuse I experienced, is no longer a mystery. I understand now there was ancestral knowledge in my body that knew to make that drum and beat it with a pencil to soothe my soul.

My first experience as an adult came through a book, which opened the gateway for me. It was a book by Carlos Castaneda, who has received some criticism for what some allege was a fictionalization of native practices. However, the wisdom was still there, and it resonated with me. I knew instinctively that there was some reality to his writings, and every time I go to Mexico, I feel at home. This would later bring me to one of my deepest connections with shamanism.

As I moved into my sacred heart space, teachers began appearing in my life, weaving in and out of my peripheral, offering their wisdom. Some teachers stayed longer than others; some became lifelong friends, imparting wisdom through our interpersonal exchange. Two of my teachers were Cherokee women who showed up at different times. One taught me the way of the Cherokee; the other taught me the way of the Q'ero of Peru. During the ensuing years, as I waited for the next teacher to appear, I began practicing in private for the most part, offering shamanic healings and journeys when I was invited. It turned out, my most valuable teacher would be the higher self I was discovering.

I worked alone and in private for about three years. And for years after that, I worked mostly in secret. I felt torn, wanting to preserve the comfort of the status quo but denying this part of myself, feeling the incongruence build. Still, the calling was strong.

We are walking a new trajectory, one that we must forge for ourselves. This path I understand and know; I have been walking it for years. Finally, I have stepped into it, to own it, as so many others have.

As the years have progressed, I have been privileged to encounter and work with many rich and beautiful traditions, including North, Central, and South American shamans, as well as spiritualists in Hawai'i and the Caribbean.

In 2010 I returned to Hawai'i, and though I never deeply studied the ways of Hawai'ians, I still embrace many of the practices. That year, I attended the Grandmothers for Peace International Pacific gathering at Volcano National Park, where I experienced a deep and meaningful connection to the Goddess of the Volcano, Pele. To this day, I follow her guidance, and she continues to call to my soul.

Now it is time to point the way on a global level so that others may forge their own deep love for all that is while honoring those who are born into the old traditions.

In 2019 I traveled to Teotihuacan. I received a deep initiation in the mystical, one that supports my identification with the way of the Toltec. This experience very clearly changed my life. While it cannot be shared publicly, as this kind of initiation is too sacred to reveal, it was earth-shattering for me. It showed me that the sacred is available to everyone who seeks with determination and a pure heart. I will be forever grateful to the amazing women who led me to this experience and to those who shared it.

In 2020, I was introduced to a community of like-minded souls who practice the ancient work of the Taíno. This group embraces anyone into their circle—one that is growing, expanding, and coming into its own. It's leader(s) have made many pilgrimages to their ancestral land of Puerto Rico to receive training that has been handed down over the generations through oral tradition. It has recently been transcribed into text and is being resurrected by the women. For more information you can contact Diane Wilson. It is my understanding that men are doing this work as well. I assisted by providing guidance to individuals who seek to connect with practices that fill in missing pieces of their ancestral knowledge. There is anthropological evidence that the Taíno were a seafaring culture that traveled all over the Caribbean and Gulf of Mexico for six thousand years. It makes sense that practices I learned from Native North, Central, and South American shamans fit nicely into the gaps in their knowledge.

While the above is a summary of my journey, it was not a direct, linear path. I came around and around to these practices, diving more deeply each time until I finally embraced it in the fullness it deserved. Your path will look differently—we each forge our own way. I invite you to consider the practices you would like to explore in your life. What do you need? What are your challenges? How can you harness presence and wholeness to enrich your life?

Journal Questions

1. Think of one way that you are attached to suffering.
2. Have you created a safe place for yourself? (Your safe place could be an emotional state or physical place.)
3. If not, how can you?

CHAPTER 5

The Original Soul Wounding

"For a seed to achieve its greatest expression, it must come completely undone. The shell cracks, its insides come out and everything changes. To someone who doesn't understand growth, it would look like complete destruction."–Cynthia Occelli

"To heal your wounds you really just need to be unafraid of what you have experienced. We have to remember that you have already been through those things and you have survived. Straight up. You know, like here we are. We've still survived. Yes, those wounds have affected us severely and have shaped our lives in all sorts of ways. But once you get the courage to reface your wounds

again. And bringing all of your intelligence of everything that you have gained through your life to, gives you the strength to dive into all of your pain and all of your wounds to reprogram yourself from within. You can't avoid it, you have to go through it."–Eshua Bolton, Didgeridoo Healer and Cermonalist

*T*o heal the wounds of our society, we, too, need to be unafraid of what we are experiencing. We are angry and disillusioned and, especially those of us in America may have observed the oppression of our friends and loved ones of marginalized races and identities. We have watched our country slowly deteriorate since the 1980s. The environment and humanity have been systematically and greedily dismantled. It is alarming. Our hard work, our good decisions have been steadily swallowed up since the mid-2000s; many of us will not have the retirements we worked for. That way of life is gone. The natural resources are under strain. Our democracy is certainly not what our forefathers (who enslaved people) envisioned. We can allow this to make us crazy. Or we can plant the seeds and grow a new society that is more sustainable for life here on earth, putting our efforts into the greater good through activism, intentional community, and radical compassion. Black Lives Matter, and for sure, all life matters, but the work of our time is to support the voices of those who have been pushed down for centuries. They deserve to be heard.

We cannot spiritually or emotionally bypass what is happening on a global level; the COVID pandemic has certainly awakened us to that. Yet, the temptation for "spiritual bypassing" is great. Many of us go through a phase where we think spiritualizing our difficulties is the only answer. Sometimes it feels impossible to live our truth, so we throw some crystals at it and tell ourselves if it is meant to be, it will happen. Any transformative model that doesn't include the struggle or doesn't involve embracing pain will not be as effective.

As we prepare to work with the sacred, stepping into this in a way that may be new to you, it is best not to use any stimulants or mind-altering substances. This includes alcohol. These substances are tools for bypassing and serve to take us out of the present and prevent us from feeling. Many of us have turned to these stimulants because we did not have spiritual venues that resonated and helped us access naturally altered states of consciousness. Some of us simply used them to forget our pain. Psychologists today believe that trauma is the original gateway drug. I invite you to commit to periods without substances for soul care, to nourish that big, beautiful heart of yours, to commit to your sanity and happiness though it means work. You can choose to drink a glass of wine a day, but I assure you, you may not go as deep if you are numbing.

I invite you to explore intentionally embracing despair and pain—individual, societal and global. By voluntarily allowing pain to move through, one can open up to beauty, love, wonder, excitement, courage, and a sense of connectedness with all of life. By allowing ourselves to experience pain *of* and *for* the world, we open ourselves up to the web of life and viscerally feel that we are not alone. This elicits a growing sense of solidarity with others and allows for a whole new sense of what our resources are and what our power is. In bypassing our pain, we risk becoming blind to these beautiful gems of wisdom and growth.

I share this path because it has been my journey. Helping others move through it involves (for the feminine) wild woman's knowledge of self-care. Some blocks and obstacles can and will arise. When they do, that is often the ego rearing its head and attempting to take control. It clings to the drama, seeking the comfort of the familiar. It is the saboteur. It is hell, a part of the collective dream or nightmare. This is now very obvious to many of us on a global level. We would like to return to the "normal" we knew, but we also know the systems and dynamics we are a part of resisting any change; staying on the paths we've traveled is comfortable.

Comfortable sounds so nice when we are afraid and alone. But we need to hold space for the blocks and obstacles that will arise, examine our triggers, truly look at the wounded self, personally and collectively. We are in the "new normal." Identify with it, validate it, and release it. Our narratives often boil down to a core fear, and though they may sound so simple, these fear stories can create a lot of suffering. It is why you will hear some say this Toltec prayer again and again, "I greet this day with all my love and no fear."

Beyond Fear: A Toltec Guide to Freedom and Joy: The Teachings of Don Miguel Ruiz offers a process for shedding fear. This process is one of our greatest allies as wild women and for the sacred masculine. We are witnessing our global structures breaking down, making way for what I believe is a huge shift for humanity. Navigating these waters requires that we seek balance. The hype we are exposed to daily offers so many avenues of fear. This fearmongering is a way to gain and maintain control. Have you ever been in a relationship that was ruled by fear? Take, for example, relationships where the messaging is: If *you pursue your dream, you will be disinherited, divorced, or in some way made an outcast.* This keeps one from developing; it keeps one domesticated. This is true on a larger scale as well. It keeps us in what Don Miguel refers to as "The Dream of Hell." This hell only exists in our minds! He explains, "The fears in one human mind become bigger when they are projected outside, [...] hell is a disease in the human mind, the whole world is a hospital." The drama arises when we are projecting our respective hells at each other. [5]

As I mentioned earlier, none of us are immune from childhood hurts and trauma. As you continue exploring your wounds, do not be surprised if you discover more pain than you expected. I am addressing this both for your healing journey and for releasing the blame. My experience led to all kinds of blame. Not only toward the abuse and abuser(s), but also toward my parents and my siblings. They were not there to protect me, and I grew to believe this was not because of a lack of awareness, rather that they chose to ignore the signs of my suffering. This need to blame and find a bad guy is driven by ego; releasing these blame stories releases our attachment to Hell in our minds.

This is not to say those who cause harm should not take responsibility for their harm. Those who have inflicted harm and wish for absolution will have to look within themselves to find that. There has been too much silence, protection of perpetrators, and impotency when it comes to bringing these matters to light. This is what the patriarchy has done. I remember being told as a middle-aged woman, when my memories first resurfaced, it is not outside of the norm. *What*? *Wow!* It may not be outside of the norm, but it sure as hell is not normal! So you see why blame is so hard to throw about? These structures of subjugation and oppression are more subtly interwoven into our society than we realize, and they affect us all.

As I moved through this processing, my healing and recovery have led me to work on forgiveness. There certainly are those who would have you believe you are harming yourself by withholding forgiveness. I do not agree with that and believe that healing comes from the discovery of our own agency. Forgiveness is often thrust upon the victim, who is told. *You will not be whole unless you forgive* as if it is a magical cure. The truth is, forgiveness is a choice, and we are empowered with the ability to forgive or not. Forgiveness is arbitrated by the victim and cannot be forced from them. Requiring forgiveness, being obligated to "turn the other cheek," is another form of spiritual bypassing. Those of us who have survived traumas may feel expected to perform forgiveness. To do so to please the outside gaze is a face of the fawning response we discussed previously. Be present with your blame. Hold space for your desire to forgive or not. And ask yourself, *Who is this in service of*? Then choose the self—always!

What is your body saying? Will forgiving bring you closure, or will it put you in some form of danger? Once you begin to have more clarity on your desires and needs, release the need to give the situation or person any more thought. When the thoughts arise, mindfully look, feel, and release. Say, "I greet this release with all my love and no fear."

Our service of self should be in the healing of the wounds and releasing any shame. Ultimately, it does not matter whose fault it was. What matters is that *it was not your fault*; your needs were not honored, and your soul was wounded. As this awareness surfaces, you may be able to connect to the disconnected pieces in your memory. Some of us may recall having nightmares as children or even notice large gaps in our memories from those years. That may now make a lot of sense. Even as children, our subconscious is doing its work, helping us to cope and release. So I suggest that we pay attention to these undercurrents. *What are they saying? And how are they protecting us?* We may forget, but we are still processing.

Though memories of trauma do not need to be retold over and over, they do come up. We cannot control this; attempting to suppress these unexpected emotional guests will lead to more pain. Even all these years later, the anger seems to come out of nowhere. It is not a simple experience but a rather complex confluence of the nervous system and emotional overload. Maybe the anger comes from a memory where you tried to tell but were not believed, or maybe it comes from remembering a confrontational moment and having your truth denied. Maybe it comes from telling a loved one and being resented for bringing awareness to your difficult experience(s). Many of us may feel forced to revisit traumas; memories and emotions will come up whether we want them to or not.

The first few times this happens, it can be extremely disorienting. Sometimes the trigger is imperceptible, and we are flung into a state of complete dysregulation without any idea why. There were years when I would see this happen in myself, watching, floating above my body, wondering where this rage came from! The triggers seemed so innocuous; I felt crazy, overreacting and lashing out over what seemed like nothing in hindsight. I know now that what was happening was an emotional flashback—my body had a visceral reaction that triggered my nervous system. My brain did not have a clear picture of what exactly the memory was. (You don't even know if the memories are there sometimes!) The truth is, it doesn't matter. The details are irrelevant: the feeling, the dysregulation, and bodily reaction give me all the information I need to work with.

Recognizing when you are locked in your trauma responses permits your self-awareness to grow as you start to see the road signs you used to miss. Unfortunately, before we hone this awareness, some of us may find ourselves acting it out as an unconscious, *compulsive repetition*. This is crazy woman and/or crazy-making behavior. Repetition compulsion is the psychoanalytic term that describes the patterns we engage in that mimic what may have been done to us. Take, for example, people who find themselves attracted to the "wrong" type for them or who somehow can only fall in love with red flags. Now, could we have made better choices? Sure. But we were not fully aware of our wounds, which our subconscious was trying to parse through. Psychologists are even beginning to agree that we all contend with *micro-traumas* that have a cumulative effect on us when they are not processed.[6] This is something that all of us experience, and the lingering effects can last throughout our lives, leaving us feeling empty and unable to understand ourselves. Getting to the deeper issues is like peeling an onion.

Try to embrace that a part of you does not feel safe and is not able to regulate. It is okay: you do not always have to be in control. Sit with the uncomfortable feelings for a moment, feel into the truth that there have been times where you were not kept safe and protected. Again, you do not need to know the details—just hold what you know in your body. Breathe, feel, and then redirect your attention to a sensory experience such as movement or music. How you choose to self-soothe is something you can control.

Recently I came across a TEDx talk by Dr. Joan Rosenburg entitled "Emotional Mastery: The Gifted Wisdom of Unpleasant Feelings."[7] In this simple, short talk, she gives solutions to building awareness by choosing to sit with an uncomfortable sensation. She names eight uncomfortable sensations and gives suggestions on how to ride the wave of emotions. She talks about how feelings are transient, often lasting 90 seconds. Of course, we know some emotions are much more enduring, such as deep grief, but this is concerning the feelings that contribute to triggers. Dr. Rosenburg named sadness, shame, helplessness, anger, vulnerability, embarrassment, disappointment, and frustration. It truly is a practice that will take time and effort. Holding these feelings does not feel good at first, but the better you get at feeling them, the sooner they seem to pass.

Many of us do not encounter this awareness of childhood wounds until well into adulthood. In my experience, survivors can sometimes feel disoriented by the flooding of awareness that comes into our lives when we are safe and stable enough to be released. If we can understand how harm transpires, we can name the harms and break trust and security. This allows us to regain our sense of trust and security in life and release pain and blame. This is not to excuse any abuse but rather to recognize that these trauma cycles often did not start with our abusers. They go further back than our memories can explore: these cycles are ancestral, this trauma is inherited. And this trauma is a result of patriarchy, white supremacy, and colonialism. I am very hopeful this collapse of our old paradigm brings about deep changes in the status quo.

It is theorized that when societies were matrilineal, abuses were not tolerated. Anthropologists have even encountered matrilineal societies that continue to exist today, finding a seemingly rape-free society.[8] What happened? How have we found ourselves in a society where one-third of women have experienced sexual violence at some point in their lifetime? This statistic is staggering. But the statistics also show 1 in 38 men will experience a completed or attempted sexual assault in their lifetimes. They are not immune to the dangers of the same patriarchy. The current difficulty in our society is that the sacred masculine cannot demand restitution, especially while being asked to hold space for the shadows of the predator. They instead have to obey the laws that often do not correct the wrongs. This has led to a mass impotency of sorts. Men must be allowed to embody their natural responsibilities—protecting, providing, righting wrongs—without being reduced to a one-dimensional paternal archetype. We too often pigeonhole the masculine into the narrow dialectic between predator and protector. The sacred masculine must also embody the balance, honoring their own feminine, inviting vulnerability, stillness, and presence as much as action and logic. This is the middle path of love and calmness, unity of the feminine and the masculine working in congruence.

A word about wounding and control subjugation: a wound does not have to look like a capital-T Trauma. We have all been molded and shaped into experiences and expectations that we did not explicitly consent to. Subtle domestication occurs through control subjugation. For example, one of the first (and sometimes hardest!) things we learn how to do in early schooling are sitting still, beinging quiet, and listening to authority figures. This prepares us to live in a society that tells us we need to produce, produce, produce without creating enough space for happiness beyond the cheap thrills found through material consumption. We know this causes stress and anxiety, with many of us living with worry, focused on the future, trying to keep up a pace that is not natural. It can cause acidity in the body, inviting disease. If we choose a minimalist way of being, we may be negatively perceived by those committed to consumerism. When we do not believe it all has to be about the almighty dollar, people may think we are nuts! Yet control subjugation means we have been expected to give up our mental and emotional freedom without even realizing it. This is a crazy-making cycle. Is it any wonder we are in the mess we are in?

Indigenous cultures in the Americas who refused to be controlled were all but wiped out in the name of manifest destiny. They were put in concentration camps we call reservations. The ancestral trauma of control subjugation is hurtful to all, even the oppressors, though the whiplash may hit future generations and leave the harm-doers relatively unscathed. These are the people who have survived. Today's descendants of these people may be the very people we turn to. They have lived in their "new normal" for generations. As I rewrite this manuscript, a short film titled "Prayer for the Earth: An Indigenous Response to These Times" was released[9]. There is currently a book in the works called *The Changing Earth: Indigenous Voices From Turtle Island* that I believe will be invaluable. It is being written by Stan Rushworth, an elder of Cherokee descent who has been teaching Native American Studies, and Dahr Jamail, a journalist who has put his career aside to contribute to this research and reporting. Their website offers: "The book emerges from how indigenous peoples' experience has given them a unique understanding of civilizational devastation, one that has endowed them with knowledge and solutions that present both radical and pragmatic responses to crises beyond anything known before."[10] What makes this book so fascinating is that they are not only looking at the original ways but also incorporating ways of adaptation and "knowledge of how to endure and persevere, no matter the odds." I get the impression there will be some surprises and new ways of looking at solutions. It will give us another way to view our circumstances, perhaps in a way that so many of us do not realize we are hungry for.

We all have an original soul wounding, some more extreme than others. In Western culture, we have no way of expressing soul loss. We say that someone has lost the will to live. There is an area of shamanism that deals directly with soul loss; it is called soul retrieval. The loss of the soul can be felt on many different levels of awareness. For example, a little over a decade ago, I experienced a traumatic event. I know a piece of my soul left me. Even with my awareness, I did not recognize the loss until I felt that little piece of my soul return. The moment it returned, I realized when and why it had left. This is not an isolated event. We all have experiences throughout our lives that cause deep grief. In our society, we may recognize on an intellectual level that we are "off," just not feeling it. We accept and hope that time will heal our grief. But we do not need to rely solely on time or traditional Western forms of healing. There are older options that originate in indigenous practices throughout the world. We honor their origins and offer thanks to the keepers of these practices.

As the original soul wounds within us are healed, we move into a more expansive form of understanding. This is not done through linear therapy, though that can be very helpful. I do not hold with the concept that in six months you will be cured, but rather engage in a cyclical healing process that allows for growth, with a focus on connecting to and expanding your intuition, thus allowing for a deeper spiritual connection to self and the natural world or even universe. We can look at this different version of healing through the work of self-love, which is a wild woman's work.

What I have discovered through my contact with medicine people, who practice spiritual shamanism, is that one is allowed to learn through experience rather than through formal education. By practicing and incorporating the above into experiential venues, we allow our participants to learn and lean into how to use both formal and informal education in the energetic/intuitive sense and to digest what has been absorbed in the formal sense of our Western intellect.

Studies have confirmed that we transmit genetic mutations to future generations. These epigenetic changes are caused by several variables; most notably, trauma is biologically inherited. Our DNA carries the wounds of our ancestors' experiences. Just as their experiences shape us, our experiences and conscious reflection can heal these evolutionary scars.

What wounds do you carry that do not belong to you? What themes recur in your fears and failures? What secrets do you keep for your ancestors? What were their fears and motivations? Which legacies do you wish to engage in? Which legacies would you like to distance yourself from? Consider processing and holding personal space for the wounds of your ancestors that you are aware of.

According to self-help author John Payne, "Science, quantum physics and metaphysics are increasingly revealing how we are all part of a greater consciousness and experiments have shown that, when critical mass is reached within a species in terms of acquiring a new skill, all other members of that species will simply adapt to the new behavior instinctively."[11] We know this is bigger than us as individuals. We and others have developed ways of changing the spiritual DNA. By changing the self, we can change our lives and communities, and even our biological DNA can be healed.

As we work on changing our biological and spiritual DNA, we must recognize that those of us who carry trauma react by either being overly independent or being codependent.

These behaviors, or ways of reacting, develop as survival strategies. Some of us develop over-independence, the need to prove to ourselves and others that we require no one to function in life, thus reducing the need to rely on others and making us feel safe and in control. On the other hand, people-pleasing codependency is a manifestation of our feelings of vulnerability within relationships and a lack of self-worth. Keeping our partners, family members, or friends happy via fawning behaviors secures our value within the relationship.

The above can be reduced to boundary issues: where do we lack boundaries, and where can we implement them? When our boundaries are too strong, we can show up as overly independent; when they are not strong enough, we slip into codependence. This we must examine from the mind of crazy woman.

To illustrate the pathology of boundaries, I will once again share a personal experience. I call this first story "Revelation" because I was shown a side of myself I did not know existed, or perhaps a better way to say this is I had forgotten.

I recently had dinner with a man I had a two-year relationship with a long time ago. This was someone I adored but who drove me crazy. After learning he had lied about a very important matter, my anger grew to astounding proportions. I remember not moving past this secret he had kept from me about himself, so I ended the relationship. After reconnecting, we met for dinner, where he mentioned that I used to become a very angry crazy. Then he informed me that at the end of our relationship, as I was kicking him out of the house, I had literally kicked him in the back. This was beyond shocking to hear about myself. I have no memory of, nor any idea I was capable of, such an act. Though I do understand the whys and that I may have been drunk (hence the lack of memory), this information cut me to the core. Honestly, I am shocked he got in touch. I certainly would not have, in his position. I admit tears stung as I tried to hold them back, hearing him share this.

I have since checked with others in my life and know this is an isolated incident. I am choosing not to feel shame over it, knowing that I carried the scars of a previous violent relationship. So much so that I feared for my life. Crazy woman builds her reactions on our experiences. It was an act of an overly independent person who could not control the behavior, so crazy woman came in and flipped a switch. Honestly, writing these words is the most challenging part of writing this entire book: the temptation to feel shame and disgust is great. But I have chosen not to be ashamed and to show myself some grace. We all are capable of doing things we would be ashamed of. It is important to name them and process these experiences to understand how to break these cycles.

When we are abused and/or abandoned at a very young age, our ability to feel safe is stripped. We lose trust. Many of us who know how to live alone come from broken homes. We choose this because to live with another, although it softens the soul, is still very scary. There is no such thing as easy love, but we must believe that love, when based on respect, requires no obligation. When respect is not being shown, or at the very least felt, then fear can creep in. The need to control, the pathology of *I do not need anyone,* is that ultra-independence I mentioned earlier. It is a defense mechanism that develops to protect us. It is all very complicated and difficult to sort out, much less look at, but I am consciously viewing this from a place of healing rather than from the wound.

This viewpoint is so important because we must be connected to our own suffering. To do so connects us to the suffering of others, thus creating compassion and empathy. When this scenario with my ex-partner happened, I was aware of my father's abandonment, but I was not yet aware of the molestation I endured as a child. Therefore I was not connected to his suffering and lacked compassion when I kicked him out.

Please be compassionate with yourself about past behaviors that are alien to your ego. There may be underlying reasons that have not surfaced just yet.

The other extreme, codependency, is also part of my past repertoire.

My next long-term relationship was with my now ex-husband. As I cleaned up my excessive drinking and became a responsible married woman, I went in the complete opposite direction. Over time, the constant need to please to feel safe in my marriage eventually removed the deep love and left only fear. The fear of abandonment and loss of security made me feel "not good enough" and bled into every area of my life. When we are insecure in a relationship and feel unworthy, it slowly eats away at our happiness and self-respect, creating anger and resentment. And there she is again, crazy woman. My ex-husband used to say to me, "Don't get so angry. It's not good for you." But you see, the marriage was eating me up inside, and I felt helpless and hopeless. This does not mean my ex was a bad person. It just means the marriage dynamics had become unhealthy.

What manifested in my marriage was most certainly codependency, likely the result of witnessing the relationship of my parents and grandparents. After all, to survive a marriage of many years used to be considered a triumph. In my case, I have little memory of the relationship between my parents, but I do remember the need to be a very good little girl after their divorce.

Again, a person who feels a loved one is threatening their security, especially a spouse, learns to do whatever it takes to keep the marriage afloat. But the cost of self-abandon is very great.

I still actively work on the above issues as a single woman. I deeply hope any future relationship(s) will have much better boundaries. I feel fortunate for the opportunity to practice boundaries with friends and family members who call me out in ways that allow me to grow. I have surrounded myself with only people who make me feel safe. I have learned to walk away from anyone who threatens my emotional security, thus avoiding the drama of the above pathologies.

Both of these pathologies, though on opposite ends of the codependency spectrum, are all about control and fixing a problem. Even now, when my options to "fix" a situation are exhausted, I lean into my frustration. So now I am looking at the contrast (what I do not want) then calling in what is desired (healthy feelings and reactions). Contrast is there to show us what we really want, even if we don't like the contrast. Allow a moment to look at the contrast before the reaction. Remember, before any negative reaction, there is a space of a few seconds for a better choice.

As we are at the end of talking about crazy, I want to expand on what I just said about choices because this is likely the most valuable thing I will discuss in this book.

Our authentic power is to turn inward into the emotional body. That is where the gap exists. Make a conscious choice to act from love. That is how you change your world. I cannot stress this enough. It is the only effective spiritual path I know of. It is the very first step in the wild woman's path. Begin with yourself.

Treat others and yourself as worthy. Choose inward love. Practice compassion for self first.

You are worthy!

Journal Questions

1.   What is one great hell that only exists in your mind? Let me give you an example I have been struggling with as I write this book: Imposter Syndrome. I recently worked out that I cannot be an imposter in my own life!

2.   As you reflect on a soul wound, begin to reflect on how you have healed that part of yourself. How did you do it? What did it feel like?

3.   If you can't think of examples for the first two prompts, then let it go. You can always revisit it later; our personal hells and wounds evolve over time.

INTERLUDE

Between

"Intent is a force that exists in the universe. When sorcerers [those who live of the Source] beckon intent, it comes to them and sets up a path for attainment, which means that sorcerers always accomplish what they set out to do."

-Carlos Castaneda, *The Active Side of Infinity*[12]

As we explore techniques that provide healing that is readily available, I would like to interject a different perspective on psychosis, trauma, and depression. Phil Borges, a social documentary photographer and filmmaker who has been documenting indigenous and tribal cultures for over twenty-five years, is also the director and executive producer of *CRAZYWISE*. This documentary explores psychological crises and how to turn them into positive transformative experiences.[13] In 2014, Borges gave a talk on psychosis and spiritual awakening, sharing statistics from the National Institute of Mental Health. At that time, the data showed that one in five of us would have at least one psychological crisis in our lifetime, one in twenty of us will become disabled, and half of the people who struggle with depression will have this crisis before the age of fourteen. We were already in a mental health crisis—imagine what these numbers look like now in a world after COVID-19.

COVID-19 and the lockdowns that accompanied it brought depression and trauma to millions. Children were especially affected, unable to touch and see their friends for months on end; many have been asked to sit for hours in front of a computer screen in remote learning. How do we help these future generations? How do we help ourselves? Lisa Miller, a professor, researcher, and clinical psychologist says, "Often depression that results from trauma can be viewed as a spiritual path because depression is the path out of trauma."[14] I hope we can show these youths that it is okay to be scared, it is okay to be angry, it is okay to be struggling with all of the various wrenches that have been thrown into our lives, and it is okay to witness and support each other through this.

In tribal cultures, most who become shamans have experienced a mental health crisis in adolescence: 75 percent experience this by age twenty-four. In mainstream society, we might see similar instances of mental health crises in folks around this age. The difference is that the tribal cultures have a cultural context for the support of these psychological crises[15]. Since the dominant cultures focus on symptom management and prescribing solutions, those suffering are rarely offered the chance to make meaning of their experience. No one in the community will come in and say, "This is a gift. You will come out the other side of this crisis a better person and a healer for your community." Tribal cultures do not stigmatize mental illness but rather offer support by those who have also been initiated by crazy. Why then would we not grasp this beautiful form of wisdom?

I always assumed my crises happened in my mid-thirties, but they did not. Remember my story as the five-year-old who made herself a drum? I was in crisis for years. As a child, I was angry and overweight. As a young teen, I was promiscuous and began using drugs. By my mid-twenties, I was a cocaine addict. Using drugs is not uncommon for people who are dealing with psychosis and trauma. All substance use is an attempt to cope with trauma. Those who are spiritually inclined may feel even more drawn to it; after all, drugs offer altered states of consciousness. For most of my twenties and early thirties, I drank like a fish. It was not until I was in a safe relationship, going to school, and feeling like I had pulled my life together that I had my first major crisis.

The first thing I did was go to a therapist and ask for drugs. Fortunately, I stumbled upon a very good therapist who treated me through Eye Movement Desensitization and Reprocessing (EMDR). She co-wrote a manual on EMDR and Chemical Dependency Treatment. Being offered the EMDR instead of psychotropic drugs, I could digest my experiences in a healthy way and at my own pace. For more information on my therapist and her techniques, you can google her name, Silke Vogelmann-Sine, Ph.D., or find her contact information in Psychology Today.

Some may need medication first to help them feel safe enough to do the internal work, and there is nothing wrong with that. Find what works for you! I was released from therapy once I had more of the answers I was seeking; my therapist and I felt confident I could continue to do the work without her.

As I continued on my own path to healing, I could not find any venues to move forward that appealed to me. Continuing with or becoming a therapist or social worker felt too restrictive for my nature. There was no cultural context for me, though I became even more deeply connected to the environment through my undergraduate degree in Human Geography, studying how humans affect the environment. I could not figure out how to find the support I craved because I, like so many, was not born into a culture equipped with those tools. As a child, I learned not to speak of my dreams, my "daydreams," or any other feelings or experiences that were beyond the understanding of those I could turn to. When I did share my inner world or broach the topic of abuse, I was told I was ridiculous and that I had an overactive imagination. The community was oblivious; hell, I was oblivious!

It was not until adulthood, six or seven years into my healing journey, still trying to figure out the next phase of my own personal healing, that I was able to find someone to mentor me. I found my first shaman through a trusted friend only because I could have a frank conversation about my own trauma. She suggested this very strange and unusual path. I knew immediately it was the right direction for me. I had done sweat lodges and been exposed enough to alternative healers; I just never knew it was a path I could take. I viewed it as my next step in therapy. It is why I have shared and continue to return so emphatically to offering the practices of shamanism as a form of connection to our primordial beingness. Now it has become so much more, bringing me great joy.

I have dedicated myself to this practice for many years, though I in no way consider myself a shaman. What I love best is finding sanctuary with nature through shamanic rituals. I want to be clear: I am not trying to indoctrinate readers into a particular way of viewing the world but rather to offer a broader view. This is not *new age* thought, but very ancient wisdom. Shamanism exists in every corner of the globe, which means you can look back at your own DNA to find your healing path if nothing else resonates.

My intention is to show a few different techniques that I have been permitted to share while also doing my best to avoid any cultural appropriation. I am also sharing tools I have developed in and for my own practice that I believe may be helpful to others. It can be difficult to find a Native practitioner who can mentor us.

The simplest method is to pick up a drum and learn some drum beats to create your own magic. We all can self-heal; just be sure you learn protective techniques any time you are connecting to other realms or dimensions. One of the safest options is to have someone hold sacred space for you. Do the best you can at honoring what is understood of the old ways. I have had people tell me I cannot perform a certain ritual or ceremony. It is true there are some traditions with closed lineages, but the tools I share have come from mentors with open traditions meant to be shared. I understand the need to honor and protect the ancient traditions; I also feel that if our egos are set aside and genuinely honoring the sacred and showing up with grace and respect, it is fine to give appropriate homage. Please do not let others shame you for manifesting your own path. I do not believe the ancient rituals and ceremonies appeared one day, but rather were developed over time out of necessity, improved upon, and collectively created. Therefore, I believe it is fine for us to create for ourselves without appropriating from others.

Because much of what I offer here are practices from my own creation, I invite you to use and develop upon them for your own personal growth. I obtained my graduate degree a decade ago by doing a practicum on healing with the Native American medicine wheel along with the family constellation work of Bert Hellinger, a family therapist whose work evolved out of Fritz Perls' Gestalt therapy. I took several workshops, doing family constellations and energy constellations that were developed by my professors. My work took these ideas one step further, incorporating both the family and energy constellation healing with modalities of nature and the wheel. Over time this has expanded and evolved.

Shamanism or animism, as some have begun to say, is not the only practice out there—it is simply the framework through which I see the world. My other practices involve daily meditation and a movement practice like yoga, swimming, or walking. My feeling is that all paths lead to Source. Find what works for you and do it!

I will also offer other easy techniques you can incorporate if you do not resonate with the shamanism pieces.

CHAPTER 6

Working with the Elements

"If the sight of the blue skies fills you with joy, if a blade of grass springing up in the field has power to move you, if the simple things of nature have a message that you understand, rejoice, for your soul is alive."

Eleonora Duse

Beginning this chapter about working with the elements, I cannot help but reflect on the fact that we are spiritual beings having a spiritual experience in a physical world that is energetic. The individual who fully grasps this concept can truly move into fully connecting to our true nature as energy beings. The universe knows who we are; it knows who everyone is.

Many have felt slight shifts away from an ill society suffering from its own imbalances and domineering patriarchy. I believe this will bring a process of renewal through the sacred medicine of healing the earth. Until we bring balance to ourselves, our planet, we will not be healthy.

We do this in simple ways: sustainable fishing, eating more of a plant-based diet, using our food as medicine (*farm*acy vs. pharmacy), and returning to the ancient ways of appreciating alchemy. If we must eat animals, let us eat those that have grazed upon the earth in a natural way, eating a healthy diet themselves. When we ingest food that has spent its life in misery, we are also putting that in our bodies. When we ingest food that has lived a healthy life in the sun and grazed upon the earth, we ingest that robust, life-giving fire. This is the way to become healthy and sustain the planet, not through mass murder, but through cultivation and caring and then gratitude towards the food for giving us strength and sustenance.

By practicing conscientious objection to the narcissistic culture, so many of us feel forced to participate in; we empower ourselves to live a life that is more in tune with who we are. The culture we have created is breaking down. This is especially true in America, where unprecedented numbers of people are unemployed right now. We must create new ways to sustain ourselves as individuals and as families, changing our priorities to those that offer more equitable opportunities. If this global pandemic has shown us anything, it is that we are all connected. The author Isabel Allende said in an interview, "What happens to a human being in Wuhan has a reflection on the entire planet."[16]

Many of us are no longer interested in "The American Dream." We see it for what it is. COVID is forcing us to ask ourselves, *how do we design a new future?* After all, we are all breathing the same air on the same planet.

Indigenous communities have long seen the lie, yet it is these communities who have been deeply affected by this virus and vulnerable to higher rates of infection and death. While they may be connected to their traditions and spiritual practice and able to greet death without deep fear, the systems of oppression and structures of power continue to wound these communities, which have already been decimated by centuries of colonization. This pandemic likely recalls previous plagues brought by settler-colonists, the ancestral trauma living inside the descendants of marginalized folks today. Yet, they continue with these spiritual practices.

For those who understand how to survive in accordance with the elements, there is no deep fear. Those who are connected to the ancestors through shamanism know that there is a lesson and a meaning to all experiences. Working with the elements is simply a way of accessing the higher realms. Staying in balance with nature through ceremonies with each of these elements, intertwining them to heal ourselves and the collective, is the work of the wild people.

Take some time to ask yourself, *how can I survive in a new and different way? What can I create? How can I make changes? What will bring me happiness in a way that will be sustainable? What makes me feel safe? What helps me to thrive?*

Shifting to alignment with self is the first step. It begins by connecting and orienting to the natural world we are such a part of. Breathe in the element of air. Stand and connect with the earth. Heal in the waters. Dance with the fire. Commune with the ethers. Dream of the life you want. This hell, this chaos, is an illusion. Dream yourself into being. You are never-ending. You have been since the beginning of time. You will continue to be until the end of time. Your form and the forms of all continue to change, but you will continue to exist as an energetic being. To put this another way, think of your calm inner voice. Is it the same voice you had as a child? Mine is. Now, as a woman in my 60s, I reflect that the same voice in my head has not changed. I see this as my energetic voice. Many of us learned the laws of thermodynamics in grade school science classes; if you recall, the first law of thermodynamics is that energy cannot be created or destroyed, only changed or transferred from one state to another. This is how we know that as energetic beings, we are endless.

We, as a colonized society, have acquired a false sense of security by building up a bank account. We work long hours to support ourselves, tying our worth to our production. We believe in the myth that if we *just work hard enough,* we can be millionaires too, amassing much more than we require. The truth is, there are systemic structures in place that control the means of production and commerce; these structures benefit a very small percentage of individuals who represent an elite hierarchy of the patriarchy that depends on us. They need us; we do not need them.

Indigenous cultures did not, and do not, require all this "stuff." They live close to the earth as stewards and partners. These are the people who live in reality, grounded in their presence and traditions. They know to ask the questions, not just *what do I gain* but *what is my responsibility to the future*?

Decolonizing wellness looks like naming the oppressive paradigms and structures in our society and unlearning the association of our self-worth with our production. It means confronting what has been done to us, acknowledging what was done to and by our ancestors, and acknowledging when we have caused harm and how the generational transmission of trauma manifests in our bodies. It is evaluating what we do with what has been done with us. It means loving our hurt parts and witnessing ourselves. It is cultivating our resilience and joy.

As COVID progresses on our planet, many of us who have relied on structures and routines are experiencing new and different emotions, perhaps even becoming aware that everything we experience is emotional. The path to transformation is to regulate these emotions, not necessarily in the ways that domestication has taught us—though intellect, control, and subjugation—but rather through discernment and acceptance using all our senses. How do we begin to do that?

There are energy centers throughout our bodies, coinciding with the regions where major nerve networks come together. Many spiritual communities rely on the Sanskrit language of chakras to understand these energy centers. While we honor the origins of chakras and the Indian cultures that have helped bring these concepts to us, we recognize that there are a variety of cultures whose heal-ing traditions discuss some form of energy centers in the body, such as the Huna tradition of Hawaii that sees energy centers as bridges of consciousness. The Hawaiian word "mana" refers to these sources of action and powers that are the basis of life itself. In all these cultures, the heart is usually the bridge, separating the lower three energy centers of the organ systems from the upper three, which deal with the ethers, space, and infinity.

As we discuss learning to connect with the elements, we will talk about each energy center with the recognition that shared insights are seen all over the world (in every corner) and that these insights are believed to have evolved separately through indigenous shamanic practices. The main way to connect to these energy centers is through movement, such as yoga and/or meditation. Georgia O'Keefe did so and said in reference to these energy centers, "I found I could say things with color and shapes that I could not say any other way—things I had no words for[17]." Since so many of us need to and love to spend time in our natural world, I am offering ways that return us to our natural balanced state by exploring the elements and connecting them to our centers. In the next chapter, I will give instructions on how to do this.

The Elements and The Energy Centers

There are seven distinct energy centers in the human body, each corresponding to a nerve plexus, anatomical regions, and one of the five elements. The first four energy centers, starting at the base of our spine and going up to the heart, are related to our internal organ systems. Earth is related to the skeletal and eliminatory systems; if you are not feeling grounded or secure, you may experience issues with your bones, joints, or large intestines. This is when we need to go to the *root* of the problem. The eliminatory system is also connected to water, including the muscular, urinary, reproductive, and lymphatic systems. Water offers the movement these systems require, including flexibility. The digestive system beginning at the mouth, is related to the fire element, which transforms food and nutrients to nourish each of the organs of that system. The respiratory systems—including the bronchial tree and the circulatory, cardiovascular, and immune systems—are related to the element of air and the heart energy center. The space element holds the endocrine and nervous systems, maintaining background processes for our bodies and the three upper energy centers.

EARTH

Every step we take is upon her. She provides all we need: grounding, support, sustenance, emotional wellbeing, and life itself. Mindfulness experts, mental health professionals, and spiritual practitioners all tout the benefits of a grounding practice. Grounding invites us to connect our energy bodies to the energy forcefield of the earth. Many may utilize common techniques such as visualizing a grounding cord or tree roots connecting the body with the earth. For others, it can be as simple as walking barefoot on the grass, gardening, or taking a long walk on a cold day. There is some scientific evidence that when we connect with the earth in this way, we are tuning our own energies to the earth's electromagnetic pulse. Those who have experienced the benefits of grounding can attest to the bodily regulation provided. We can lower our blood pressure, heart rates, and stress levels by integrating grounding into our lives. If you have not yet experienced this or have wondered if you were doing it right, I invite you to try these grounding instructions.

Seated Grounding:

To ground through the *root center* while seated, bring your awareness to the place where your body connects to the ground. Then simply visualize running energy down your spinal column through your tailbone or feet.

Lying Down Grounding:

You can also connect through the tailbone while lying on your back. Visualize a cord coming from your tailbone, down through your body, and into the earth, attaching you. I like to visualize wrapping a cord around the earth's core.

Standing Grounding:

Bring your feet hip-distance apart and stand firmly on the balls of your feet, lifting your toes off the ground. Feel the four corners of your feet as they meet the Earth. After dropping your toes back down, begin to run your energy into the ground. Do not be surprised if, at some point, you feel a return of energy.

I invite you to close your eyes while using any of these methods, but it is not necessary for you to receive the benefits of grounding. Many of us with a trauma history feel vulnerable with our eyes closed. Find what works for you! If connecting directly to the earth feels difficult, try connecting to an animal that has a den in the earth, such as a wolf, fox, or bear. Even connecting to your dog while sitting upon the earth is a deeply grounding practice. A cat on the lap works as well; after all, cats are famed for their sense of balance. Animals do not need us to balance them. We need them to balance ourselves.

Those of us who live in cities (or even those who do not but who spend more time indoors than they would prefer) must remember that even our dwellings were made from resources found on this earth. Stand with your back against a wall or plant your bare feet on a tile floor or even lie in the bathtub. You can find her anywhere!

Once we connect to the earth, we must listen. What we need can be found if we know where to look. Wild woman listens to her body and keeps her own counsel. When we are in pain, it is important to note the root, the base, represents our present mental condition and how it affects our bodies. Here the saying "getting to the root of the problem" holds special validity.

All the energy centers have corresponding colors. Your root energy is associated with the color red and spins in a counterclockwise direction. This energy center holds perceived survival needs. When it is in balance, you feel grounded and safe. It is related to the endocrine glands and adrenals. The associated areas of the body are the base of the torso, the legs, and the feet. Health problems related to this energy center may be skeletal and joint-related. The earth is associated with the sense of smell.

WATER

The water codes carry so much. We use water to purify and cleanse. It is also the element most closely related to sex. We heal well with water because we carry so much of it in our bodies. It speaks fluidly and fills things up; it embraces us and relieves us of the weight of gravity. People from around the world and across cultures have sought water's unique capability to restore, relax, focus, and engage our senses. In this way, water makes the perfect medium to inspire, foster, and cultivate mindfulness, creativity, and overall happiness. In many parts of the world, indigenous groups are at the forefront of ecological conservation activism. Water has been used as a healing source for all indigenous cultures. "Indigenous peoples regard the inland waters, rivers, wetlands, sea, islands, reefs, sandbars and seagrass beds as an inseparable part of their estates. As well as underpinning social and economic well-being, Indigenous people's relationship with waters, lands and its resources is crucial to cultural vitality and resilience."[18] Maori activists in New Zealand succeeded in obtaining the legal recognition of personhood for a river sacred to the people native to its banks. This is just one example of how we can appreciate the wisdom of these communities who are well aware of the magic of water and who fight every day to protect it.

How can you balance yourself with the waters? It is always best to immerse oneself. For me, it has always been the sea, especially the Caribbean Sea. There is nothing like connecting to the fish, the turtles, and the dolphins in warm clear waters. If total immersion is not an option for you, wading in a small stream or walking past a water fixture also works! If all else fails, dancing in the rain or taking a hot, mindful shower can do the trick.

As you work with the element of water, think about the sacral energy center. It is located in the womb space, the sacred space we all carry inside our abdomen, regardless of anatomical womb-like features. For folks without a physical womb, it is located three fingers below the navel. We all carry emotion in our pelvic region. We also carry creativity here, not only the power to create but creative energy itself. It is also called "the dwelling place" and deals with the core feelings of the self. *What are we attracted to? What do we find distasteful?*

The human relationship with water is so inseparable because we consist of over 70% water when we are born,[19] which is about the same percentage of water on Earth. Dr. Wallace J. Nichols, the creator of The Blue Mind Company, developed his Blue Mind concepts from his research and career as an oceanographer. Dr. Nichols compiled strong evidence across fields of science and behavior that shows how water can help us live happier and healthier lives. He documented a wide spectrum of benefits, including increased creativity and flow, improved focus, increased calm, and improved physical and emotional wellbeing, as well as overall connectedness.[20]

When working with the sacral center, we visualize the disk spinning clockwise in a bright shade of the color orange. The location of this energy center is the center of the pelvis, in the region where our nerves travel through our sex organs and lower intestines. Issues related to this area are intimacy and emotions. When it is in balance, you have a healthy sexuality. Associated health problems are often reproductive. Water, with its hydration and adaptability, is also related to the sense of taste.

FIRE

Just like earth and water, it gives us life. Without the sun kissing the earth, how would we eat? It provides light and safety and is a catalyst for change. Fire is birth and death. We use a flame for cooking and nourishing; there is a reason why the hearth was the center of the home for so many centuries. We eat and breathe fire through photosynthesis, the process through which plants capture the sun's energy and convert water, carbon dioxide, and minerals into oxygen and organic compounds. This incredible process provides the air we breathe. Many feel the pull to stare into the flames and watch the colors and shapes dance. It is so mesmerizing. Fire ceremonies are typically held at night around new and full moons. In most medicine circles I have been involved with, the pit is always the center. Even today, campfires are set up that way. Fires provide wonderful opportunities to connect with spirit or simply to connect. Fire allows us to remember who we are, in some cases to re-remember.

Since 2012, solar flares in our planetary system have increased due to our changing sun. University scientists have theorized that these solar flares are causing psycho-active experiences that create hallucinations in our brains. Some believe the ionic ratio change in our brains is actually opening doors within the pineal gland, thus allowing us to have multi-dimensional experiences. As research on this topic develops, we will continue to learn about solar flares, but it is interesting food for thought!

Speaking of food, it is important to note, "most people's pineal glands are heavily calcified. So much so that they show up as a lump of calcium during an MRI.... Calcification is the buildup of calcium phosphate crystals in various parts of the body.... It appears from the latest research that this may be the cause of most disease. From arthritis, to stroke, from cancer to back pain. Due to the...standard american diet..." And flouride. More on the pineal later.

None of the elements exist in a vacuum. They are all interconnected: the earth and air are required components of an active flame. I invite you to observe how you are already working with the element of fire and identify how you might harness these with intention, perhaps something as simple as lighting a candle for the healing and well-being of yourself and others. The small rituals that you may already incorporate into your life, such as working with the flame as you cook yourself a nutritious meal. You don't need a giant bonfire to connect with this element. One fun trick I like to use is to take photos of the fire, then look at the still shots of what you saw, zooming in and out to appreciate the colors and textures.

The energy center for fire is the abdominal core, where our nerves intersect in the solar plexus, right below the sternum, where our diaphragm sits under our lungs. This is where we carry our power, how we exert control over others, but more importantly, our empowerment, the recognition of our complete responsibility to ourselves, and our sense of protection. As we work with this energy center, imagine the color yellow spinning counterclockwise. When it is out of balance, one may notice issues in the organs related to digestion, low self-esteem, and lack of energy. If it burns too dimly, we do not honor ourselves; too brightly, and we do not honor the boundaries of others or society. When this energy center is in balance, we have healthy social roles, are conscious of our worth, and maintain healthy boundaries. Fire, with the light it provides, is related to our sense of sight.

AIR

The breath of life. It makes us free: we are limitless when we practice our breathwork. The blowing air can calm us. It is cleansing; it brings changes. How often have you heard someone say "just breathe"? It sounds so simple, yet that is the most powerful tool in your toolbox.

This is the element we have the most conscious control over. Yet, it is also the element we do not have to think about, as breathing is an autonomic process regulated by our nervous systems and the energy centers they travel through.

Working with this element is so important because it offers a way to regulate our well-being. Practicing breathwork, such as yoga and meditation, or simply learning brief breathing techniques enhances stress reduction and relief by taking us out of our heads. Singing relies on the manipulation of breath through the vocal cords.

Here are some other ways to connect with the element of air: dancing with fluid movements, paying attention to the wind, watching the clouds move across the sky. We can light incense or a smudge stick and observe the smoke rising through the ambient air. Notice how this feels. It can shift the energy in a tense room because this element engages our sense of smell, pulling us into the present and our bodies. If you are stressed, try to observe your breath first, counting as you inhale and counting as you exhale. Find a length of time that is comfortable for you and your body, inhaling for a period and then adding a little more time to the exhale. The longer exhale helps calm the nervous system and heart, thus facilitating a sense of connection and safety. We are looking for low and slow breath regulation, not necessarily big deep breaths. When we meditate, we do not take deep breaths, but we do take conscious breaths. When I was first learning to meditate, I would simply tell myself, "I am breathing in, I am breathing out." With this simple awareness technique, you can change the entire state of your being. It is a good little mantra until other mantras come along.

Air is the element of the heart center, the fourth energy center. Of course, this center is all about love. Breathing and spiritual breath work consciously expand this center. Every spiritual tradition works with the heart and our connection to everything. This has been true since the beginning of humankind. It is why I have said over and over *we are all connected*. But it is not only the spiritual traditions that say this. Science tells us this through life science, astronomy, and quantum physics; it comes up through matter, energy, and all of life down to the tiniest organism because connection exists in every level of universal organization.

Imagine your heart center to be a bit to the right of where you think it is. It does not sit on the far left. Its disc spins clockwise in the color green. Emotional issues related to this energy center are depression, self-doubt, and pessimism. The corresponding body areas are the heart, lungs, blood, circulatory system, shoulders, and arms. When it is imbalanced, one may notice issues related to the thymus gland, heart, and respiratory system. When it is in balance, you allow for unconditional love, embracing life as it is, embodying vitality. Working with the heart center plays an essential role in stress reduction.

ETHER

The void. The space that is all around, that exists within, outside of us, and in all the in-between spaces. It is the medium through which the light of the spirit travels. It is also the void of darkness. This element represents the upper three energy centers in the body, the throat, third eye, and crown.

Menas Kafatos and Deepak Chopra wrote a book, *You Are the Universe: Discovering Your Cosmic Self and Why It*

Matters. Deepak Chopra mentions the split between the spiritual and the scientific in this book, asserting that science is based on a subject/object split or a separation, with humans being separate from the universe. He believes this separation has contributed to the suffering of war, poverty, environmental destruction, etc. He uses the example of the same electricity that creates thunder and lightning in the sky being responsible for the synapses that fire in our brains on a microscopic level to create our thoughts! To think that we are separate from the environment and the world we live in is preposterous—to use his words, "it is psychotic."

The fifth energy center, the throat center, deals with how we listen and speak. It is this area we use most consciously in our work, in our day-to-day life, as communication. It is sound and speech and voice without sounds, such as writing or sense of self. It is a connection, social well-being, and co-regulation. Our vocal cords vibrate to create the words we speak aloud; emergent studies on polyvagal theory have identified that these vibrations may also help to increase vagal tone, an aspect of our nervous system responsible for cultivating feelings of connection and safety. This is why chanting and singing are so prevalent in rites of purification and expressions of human joy. I do not know anyone who does not appreciate music; it soothes our soul. It is uplifting and can bring us to tears.

Our emotions and how we express them are also linked with this center, located in the throat but also associated with the neck, mouth, and thyroid. As you sit with this energy center, visualize it in blue, spinning counterclockwise. When it is imbalanced, health problems may manifest in the thyroid, speech, and endocrine system. When it is balanced, one is more likely to have clear direction and communication, and one can speak their truth.

Next is the third eye, the sixth energy center, located behind the eyebrows, between the eyes, at the pineal gland. It is associated with images, internal viewing, psychic abilities, memories, and dreams. The wild woman's work is learning to identify, connect, and listen deeply to the messages that come. When we do not listen, we bring difficulties into our lives.

The pineal is related to both fire and ether. It is a crucial part of the endocrine system, producing serotonin and melatonin along with controlling bodily processes like growth, metabolism, and hormones, including those that are responsible for sexual development. But to me, the most interesting function of the pineal is its ability to unlock our third eye. The pituitary is considered the master gland because it controls the growth of other glands and organs and is often referred to as the gland of reason. But the pineal holds a special place in conjunction with the third eye because it plugs into the photoreceptors of the brain. The pineal is lined with tissue made up of pinealocytes; these tissues are similar to the rods and cones in the retina of your eyes. Descartes referred to the pineal gland as the seat of the soul, as the anatomical study of the brain emerged during his life. He realized its importance in seeing, conceptualizing, understanding the self in relation to others, awareness of consciousness, and the role of dreams, which were all important topics in his major philosophical works. It is our connection to the psychic and spiritual realms.

Philosophers throughout history saw that it is capable of individual awakening. But what if collectively we learn that we do have a consciousness beyond the physical?

Death being "the end" is a philosophy that has not been proven. Somehow ancients knew this too, as evidenced by their scriptures and ancient artifacts that have been discovered. The third eye is shown with a pinecone shape above it on many Egyptian artifacts; of course there is no surprise that it is an accurate description of the pineal gland. Buddha and Christ are depicted in artistic relics with halos glowing around their foreheads. This gland, along with the third eye, is even mentioned many times in the Bible, as seen in this line of scripture, "The light of the body is the eye: if therefore thine eye be single, thy whole body shall be full of light."—Matthew 6:22, King James Version

This third-eye energy center is visualized in a violet color, spinning clockwise. Related issues are dedication (or lack of) to the spiritual path; body areas are the senses. When it is balanced, one is calm and focused, trusting their wisdom and intuition. When it is out of balance, health problems related to the senses may manifest. Know that you can tap into this energy center through meditation, shamanic drumming, lucid dreaming, and more. It is our present psychic condition.

Our seventh and last major energy center is located at the crown of our heads. It is where thought, consciousness, and awareness take form. Learning, intelligence, and integration come into play here. This energy center connects us to Source, the energy of all that is. It is the center of a "thousand petals," *enlightened awareness.*

This energy center represents spiritual separation, as well as connection to the divine. The related body areas are the brain, pineal gland, and nervous system. Health problems are separation from source, dissociation, and spiritual bypassing. When the crown energy center is in balance, we are aligned with unity consciousness and connection to the divine. It is here that one feels the fullness of spiritual practice, whether it be through yoga, meditation, or the dance of the whirling dervish. It is also a means of attaining altered states of consciousness. The associated color transcends our understanding; I like to visualize it like a shining star or a bright crystal emitting a prism of light. Ether/space offers limitless expansiveness. All we have to do with the three higher energy centers is listen and perceive the subtle messages.

The five elements discussed here comprise all the matter in the physical world and help us build a bridge to our higher self by building awareness of and working with our nervous systems. This transformation often starts with a simple observation of self. Notice where we end, and others begin: *What kind of space do I take up? How do I show up for others? How do I show up for me?*

Receiving is a form of spirituality that is co-creative. So often in our society, we are taught that receiving has a cost because we live in a capitalist world. But there is no cost to receiving from the universe; there is only abundant love, which leads us to self-unification. As we learn to receive in this original way, we choose to unlearn the fear of survival and the price of receiving.

In the above description of the energy centers and their correspondence to the elements, you may recognize pieces of it that are reminiscent of the ancient wisdom of the Kundalini, a form of divine feminine energy that originated in Hindu culture. The same energies that run through our bodies also run through the body of the earth.

Using the above and what we discuss in the next chapters will allow you to operate on your own authority, thus gaining a sense of who you are in relation to all that surrounds you. If this path is new, your life will change based on who you are and how you are feeling. I cannot stress enough how important it is to understand who you are.

Journal Questions

1. How can you live a life that is more in tune with who you are?
2. Make a list of your core beliefs.
3. Make a list of how you can intentionally change your life.
4. Make sure your beliefs and your intentions are in alignment.
5. Take time to ask yourself:
6. How can I survive in a new and different way?
7. What can I create?
8. How can I make changes?
9. What will benefit me, bring me happiness in a sustainable and reasonable way?
10. What makes me feel safe?
11. What helps me to thrive?

CHAPTER 7

Mojo Rising: Embracing our Wild Natures

"I touch my own skin, and it tells me that before there was any harm, there was miracle."

- adrienne maree brown

Realizing that you can step into a much bigger life can be quite daunting. I felt so far away from the woman who found it remarkably easy to pick up her mojo and get to living! I grieved that missing part of myself and sometimes felt angry that I could not turn it on! Triggers are going to happen; the important thing is how we deal with them. If you desire a more abundant and happy life, your cultivating efforts must begin in a rooted place within you. We can create from a place of pain or trauma, especially when we need to be witnessed. But efforts towards transmuting these shadows into wisdom hold more power if based on your wholeness rather than your wounds, the very same place of miracle in the quote at the beginning of this chapter. By holding our triggers as an opportunity to sit with the feelings *in our bodies* and asking *Why am I triggered?* We are able to go deeper. Of course, if you have been on this path for a while, you are familiar with this place of sitting and noticing. I learn something new each time I dedicate myself to this fundamental practice. We are never too advanced to revisit the basics; take what you need from this and leave the rest.

Once we've done some work of looking at the what and why of ourselves and our wounds, as we did in earlier chapters, we have the opportunity to tap into the joy of being (more) at home in our bodies. I am learning to go deeper into the wisdom of my body, even when I have felt betrayed by my body. This is how we get down to that core, the root. We know that crazy does not fit in with who we truly are. Crazy lives in the mind. Working through this teaches us to be much less reactive as a whole. Each time we get to that place of *Ah, that's why!* We feel our bodies settle. We begin to do only what feels good in our being. This may include a geographical move. We all have our own happy place. I had someone once tell me there is no such thing as a geographical cure. For some of us there is, as long as we recognize that our inner work will travel with us!

*"do not choose the lesser life. do you hear me. do
you hear me. choose the life that is. yours. the life
that is seducing your lungs. that is dripping down
your chin."–Nayyirah Waheed*

When we flow with what feels right in our bodies, that's
when the mojo starts to rise. We give ourselves permis-
sion to live; we stop apologizing all the time. We stop the
"good girl" pleasing behavior that we know really does not
align with our needs, instead inviting into our lives only
those who honor us from a place of authenticity rather
than superiority. And as my mojo rose, I realized I did
not have to be the dried-up, middle-aged woman society
expected me to be. Found within my connection to the sexy,
natural parts of myself were the woman who danced with
nature and allowed life to be celebrated and a sovereignty
guiding me towards joy and pleasure. Wow! Baby, that is
pure unadulterated MOJO—and a direct line to the divine
feminine within.

If you have never felt some of these things, this is your
opportunity to start exploring them. This is also an invitation to hold space for the erotic, embracing all the sensual
abundance that we carry. For me, as I continue building an
amicable friendship with my body, it feels like returning
to a younger, more vibrant me. Oh, how I love this girl!
I recognize her. I admit I was afraid she was gone. I had
Lasik surgery decades ago and the first time I caught my
own reflection in the mirror, I thought I was seeing an
old friend! And then I realized, it was me in the mirror,

beholding my own face without glasses. I had the same feeling when I felt my mojo returning.

We, of course, cannot discuss mojo and the return of it without talking about sex and pleasure, as both are primal and so good for our souls. I want to recommend a fabulous book by adrienne maree brown, whom I quoted at the beginning of the chapter: *Pleasure Activism: The Politics of Feeling Good.* This book, in my opinion, has something for everyone, despite being largely written for femmes of color. What I love best about the book is her inclusion of advice on a host of subjects: managing triggers, negotiating consent, and how to get more deeply in touch with and in love with your own body. Plus, she offers what she calls "hot and heavy homework" at the end of each chapter. Good stuff—you won't be disappointed!

So, what is mojo? Looking up the origins of mojo, sources say it is West African, possibly from the Fula word "moco'o" which means "medicine man." It is very old and was brought to America by enslaved Africans. Their modern-day descendants, Hoodoo and Conjure practitioners, have their own modern-day meaning within their traditional religions. The popular concept of mojo has been vernacularized to mean "personal magic." Every time I begin to discuss mojo, someone will ask, "What do you mean by mojo?" And I think, *Wow! I know what it is, but how do I describe it?* This is what I came up with:

*Mojo is the radiance in all of us. It includes the
ability to express that radiance to others, bringing
it out of ourselves and into the world around us
not only through words and actions but also by
the way we carry ourselves.*

You may be familiar with the way it has been described
in sports. A recent Washington Post article quoted a 1999
New York Times Magazine: "All the televised football in the
world can't compensate suburban men for their lost warrior
mojo." There are a variety of factors that contribute to our
sense of having our mojo, such as self-love, community support, embodiment, peak experiences, a sense of belonging,
and a sense of safety. So many of these experiences depend
not on self-regulation but on co-regulation, the relational
experience of finding and holding safety with another. As
mentioned at the beginning of this book, if our wounds
occurred in a relational context, doesn't it also make sense
that our healing would as well?

When COVID upended our lives, many of us did not
expect to be isolated and far from our loved ones; we had
chosen to live far away and have separate lives in this glo-
balized world. Researchers have found this especially true
for men, who tend to lack the community networks women
are socialized to build from a very young age.

When the world of bars and sports events was canceled
due to the risks of airborne virus droplets, many experienced unprecedented isolation and likely needed deeper
connections to bridge the physical distance. Beyond the
gendered patterns of our social lives and virus responses,

it can simply be a challenge to find friends and community in adulthood, especially as the structures of academic institutions and extracurricular activities have faded away. Journalist Samantha Schmidt summarized some theorized origins: "The lack of vulnerability in male friendships is rooted in a misogynistic, homophobic culture that discourages emotional intimacy between men. But it is also part of a culture that does not value adult friendship in general." Patriarchy has poisoned vulnerability in an attempt to convince us that it is a sign of weakness rather than the badge of radical courage it can be. How do we remedy this? We practice being vulnerable every day—first with ourselves, then slowly with others as we grow comfortable with the feeling. We tell our friends we love them—even when it feels awkward or we feel internalized shame arises. This is vulnerability in action.

This conscious vulnerability helps us practice emotional risk-taking and learn what it feels like to have our vulnerability witnessed with love, bringing us closer to those feelings of safety that are so important and that increase our mojo. Vulnerability can feel like an obstacle if we do not yet have healthy methods of self-soothing. Many of us were not taught to self-soothe properly as children, to find ways to help us feel safe or redirect the mind when necessary. I invite you to explore what self-soothing you might need in your life now or may have needed as a child.

How do we find the co-regulation our healing requires? Working with our inner child is one form of co-regulation. We offer our inner child the safety of an adult who will be there for them in a way that may not have occurred in the past. When one is ready to begin working on an intimate relationship with another, but this "other" is unavailable, we can step into this self-driven approach to work with parts of ourselves and/or work with the elements, for in the shamanistic, animistic view of the world, we are never truly isolated if everything has a soul or a spirit.

We have learned through domestication that the elements are somehow inhospitable, that wildness is to be feared. We have been taught we must challenge and overcome the elements. Yet, many of our first sensory experiences happen with nature. This lie has helped stratify the separation between our bodies and the earth. By falling in love with the elements, we tap into our inner knowing; we understand *we are the authority* and our own medicine. Those of us who lived alone when the pandemic hit have been forced to spend more time in solitude, many finding what at first felt like restriction has become a gift. This time of forced aloneness offered many an opportunity to observe our own development through our respective tribulations.

I always see through shamanic eyes, only because that is what makes the most sense to me. It makes me feel empowered rather than powerless when it comes to healing, including the healing of the collective. By often practicing with my third eye and higher self, I can receive clarity into any number of life's challenges, including the imbalances we have been discussing in this book. It is through this practice I met a distorted distrust of self behind my fear of being alone. It was simply another shadow. The discovery once embodied on a cellular level, revoked its hold over me. We know our DNA holds the blessings and dreams of our ancestors, as well as their fears and traumas. When we begin to break generational cycles, we are actively changing our spiritual DNA, creating new pathways for the future. Working with the energies offered in shamanism, one never truly feels alone. Having the support of the elements and all they embody allows for a childlike wonder that can be transferred to the exploration of our inner child. Nature is my friend; nature is our friend.

What gifts are you developing now for your inner child? What gifts would you like to provide to your descendants? Cultivating this innocence of the inner child is a rekindling of our wildness. For me, the word wild is a rejection of norms and expectations imposed upon us, both individually and collectively.

By letting go of the norms and expectations, I have built an intimate connection with myself that allowed me to be softer and kinder to her, understanding and accepting the mistrust of self. I am hopeful that my distrust of others will soften in time as well. The wisdom of Brené Brown sums it up best: "Strong back, soft belly, and wild heart."

Be aware that there may be those who will feel threatened by your raised vibration and your joy. Others may see your mojo and become negative, especially as we stop fitting so neatly into the spaces meant for us in their lives. I am speaking from experience regarding the above scenarios; we have all had those moments of joy only to have it punctured by another. Try not to let it deflate you; if it does, examine your past dynamic with this person or people. *What might be triggering them?* It is not yours to solve or manage, but sometimes a deeper look can help us reassure ourselves it is not our fault. There is a quote you hear a lot in self-help: "The people who are most upset by you setting boundaries are those who benefitted from your having none." *How have your boundaries changed? Who benefitted from them (or the lack thereof) in the past? Who benefits from the revised version?* While the people who depended on our lack of boundaries were likely the primary beneficiaries before, honest and authentic boundaries in relationships benefit *all* parties as we can show up as ourselves.

When we are in a state that is on a higher vibrational level, we tend to think we can maintain it because it takes so much work to get there. But that is not the case. Mojo, like anything else, must be continually nurtured. Repression can block mojo. By creating boundaries, we learn to set a standard for what we want and what we will tolerate. The key ingredient is maintenance. The lessons will continue to present themselves until we learn them. Removing someone from your life is not about punishing them; it is about honoring your needs, your desires, and your commitment to who you want to be, who you truly are! Look at your patterns and ensure you do not repeat those that do not serve you in a healthy way.

I invite you to witness yourself and explore what taking an emotional risk may look like: perhaps slowing down, being mindful, and embracing stillness if you bypass through busyness; perhaps embracing movement if you bypass through stillness and spirituality. Tap into your bodily intuition. Remember the wonder of who *you* are and hang onto that wonder no matter what life hands you. When life hands you challenges, and you screw up by not honoring the self, simply vow to do better. Center on your potential, not your flaws.

Retrieving Your Mojo

*What do we do when we know we have
lost our mojo?*

Mojo comes and goes. Sometimes we are so charismatic that others are drawn to us. At other times, we feel so far from ourselves that we lose our mojo, sometimes for years. For some, it is never regained. When we lose this magic inside of us, it is usually because we have been giving it out to sustain others. We must retain our power to ensure it is available to nourish our souls. Our life energy cannot sustain those other than ourselves, nor should it. We cannot feel, cope, and experience for others, even if we are parents or caregivers. This kind of enabling can be a form of control as we rob our loved ones of their opportunities for growth. The best we can do is be present with them and help them co-regulate.

Control and possessiveness are more subtle and commonplace in relationships than one might think, often used in misguided attempts to manipulate love, leaving us feeling like we are on shaky ground with partners, family members, or friends. It does not feel good to be controlled: this kind of dynamic can turn us into objects and pleasure into a transaction. Sometimes the people in our lives are demanding this kind of controlled love from us to meet their own needs. As the adage says, *hurt people hurt people.*

But the fact that someone was not offered the real care they needed does not excuse controlling behavior. This is a deep systemic problem in our culture. Relationship skills that are modeled for young people are patronizing and paternalistic. Patriarchy and heteronormativity impose their shadows on our relational dynamics; it is up to us to name them and refuse to participate.

If you are tolerating or enabling this kind of behavior in your life, this is an invitation to take a look. *Does your life reflect and align with your values, with who you are?* If you fear what your loved ones would say if you told them your experience, that might be a very good reason to explore it. I had to look at my own codependency and how it got in the way of my mojo. The work of unlearning enmeshed attachments and codependence is hard and felt counterintuitive to everything I had known previously about relationships and love. Love cannot show up for us the way we need it to in any relationship that is based on control. Permitting ourselves to fall into this cycle causes a loss of self-love and self-respect, and then you-know-who shows up: crazy. Crazy woman was my sign that my nervous system needed some love and that the story I believed about myself did not reflect my truth. We all have our stories, and ultimately, that's all they are: stories. We are not just a character in it; we are writers! Our job is to change the script.

While it may feel scary to be in the writer's seat, striving to rewrite the narrative from a place of agency, we welcome the dissonance and acknowledge the complexities of holding contrasting truths simultaneously. Any form of the above alchemy involves being in consciousness with the self as an act of intimacy, one that creates a love that you do not have to control in any way.

Because there is no need to control or protect myself, the clarity can be allowed to shine through. As you learn to trust yourself and to thrive under your own sovereignty, then your mojo will begin to return. The journey to wholeness is not about discarding our shadows and wounds but about integrating them with our awareness that we are still going to experience triggers. Our wounds are still going to become inflamed when they are exposed. A scab does not heal into a scar overnight. This journey of dealing with trauma is a lifelong commitment. This is part of the reason some of these tougher shadows, like rage and abandonment, stay with us; our bodies bear the scars of these wounds even long after they have healed on the surface. Do not despair—the triggers may never fully disappear, but they mostly lose their intensity over time as we learn to give ourselves what we need.

So, how do we know we are missing a part of ourselves? It can be hard to discern at first, but we can start by noticing how our own energies ebb and flow. When we know, we know because we can remember what that bliss of life felt like, moments where we felt alive, at home, and in our bodies. We can all recall these juicy moments—even if they feel hard to recall in the mind, your body knows what they felt like. Let's talk about how to bring them out of your memories and into your awareness. Then, we will talk about cultivating these experiences and manifesting this state of being.

When I allude to these moments of bliss, I am reminded of the concept of *peak experiences*. I hope you are all familiar with these wonderful memories, such as that moment when you lay eyes on something or someone that lights up the world. Sometimes it's a moment; sometimes it's a place, sometimes it's a fantastical dream you are all too sorry to wake up from. If an experience does not immediately come to mind, do not despair. I will share some examples that may sound familiar.

My fondest peak experience happened when I was in my early forties. I was riding a horse that had been given to me by a friend who had moved. Kimo was a very finely bred Arab who was trained as a dressage horse. I learned so much from him, but this moment was the pinnacle of our relationship. We were cantering through a grove of macadamia trees in Hawaii. I could tell he was happy to be there. In my mind, I had a thought to go in a certain direction. The wild thing is, the horse responded to my thoughts! Now maybe I was unconsciously sending cues; we will never know, except to say I am not a sophisticated enough rider where that kind of communication is standard. The point is he, and I had a moment of visceral and spiritual connection. Every thought I had, he answered by physically delivering the action. It was pure bliss. I find myself returning to this moment in my mind's eye time and again.

List or even write a story around your peak experiences. If you do not have full memories sitting in your mind, play with writing down experiences that have felt good (or you think might feel good) to you, filled you with joy, allowed you to be in your body, made you feel safe and loved. These experiences also come in seed form, growing from tiny moments of magic. I learned a new concept the other day: the idea of glimmers. A glimmer is the opposite of a trigger, something that makes us feel safe and content. Glimmers, for me, are moments of deep happiness. They come through looking at the ocean, looking at the sky, and moments of gratitude. It's not that they weren't present in the past when I may not have been feeling as whole; I just could not see or feel them as easily. Now I notice my glimmers several times a day! And we have everything we need to bring us back into this glimmery space inside us in our day-to-day lives by befriending ourselves and the planet.

When we work with the elements, we allow nature to nurture us and, in turn, nurture the nature around us. By surrendering to this wisdom, we can cultivate the balance we seek inside ourselves. As you practice connecting to our bountiful Earth, you may find yourself with some plant, animal, or spirit companions. These kindred spirits normally choose you; it is not you who chooses the companion. These allies can change or be added. Be open to that which may come in unexpected forms. In my experience, they do seem to remain with us once they have chosen us, though not always in the forefront. Many cultures resonate with companion spirits. This is why they are called spirit allies or familiars. Please note that the concept of "spirit animals" is largely considered cultural appropriation today, and Native American communities have asked that we not commodify their culture.

When I was young, just approaching puberty, I was swimming across a channel of the Mississippi River in eastern Iowa with my aunt. It was a long swim, so when I got to the other side, I tried to touch the bottom. I went under, and as my foot touched what felt like a rock, I heard a very angry and loud sound, startling me to swim away. I had disturbed a snapping turtle's rest. It came up and bit me on the top of my right foot. Fortunately, the injury was not as severe since I was swimming. Fifty or so years later, I still have the scars. When we are chosen by an ally or a guide, we don't often understand the meaning, even if it bites us on the foot! This turtle experience led me to a lifelong love of turtles. Sea turtles, for me, are shamans of the seas, for they carry deep and powerful tools of navigation and survival.

What is an experience you have had that may have been perceived as difficult or negative but that you later, or maybe even just now, realized was actually a gift? Learning to pause and see the gift is part of cultivating mojo.

Journal Questions

1. How can you be more consciously vulnerable?
2. Does your life reflect and align with your values, with who you are?
3. How do you want to change your story?
4. How are you going to rewrite the script? Remember, it's not written in stone. Go for it. Just write what you want right now.

CHAPTER 8

Trust, Lineage, and Responsibility: A Threefold Path to the Future

*B*efore COVID hit, in the first drafts of this book, I had written, "I believe we are going to see a big shift happen in the next 20 to 50 years. I believe our grandchildren will see their grandchildren grow up in a much healthier world than the one we inhabit today." Taking stock of what a strange year 2020 was, I believe this even more now. Each of us, in our own way, is a part of the solution to humanity's problems. How large a part is up to us. Do we create a genuine elevation of our consciousness and divine connection to the planet? Or do we just sit in the status quo of the "new normal" and hope that this all just rights itself on its own?

I really dislike the term "the new normal," the implication that life post-COVID looks like isolation without community. The truth is "normal" never existed. American society has had some serious shadow work to do for a few centuries now; there are more systemic harms being imposed on folks than we realize. Some of this has come to light during the pandemic, but there is much more to heal. There seems to be a black and white, all-or-nothing polarity to American consciousness sometimes. I invite you to practice holding the black and the white and all the shades in between. The answer is not isolating ourselves entirely from our communities but engaging with a harm reduction mentality to meet our mental and physical health needs while mitigating risks with knowledge.

The reframing and reformations that we need will come through the people, through small businesses, through change-makers and innovators. Most importantly, it will come through the way we parent our children. We know we have a huge problem with technology and algorithms. Those who created those algorithms have admitted they are overwhelmed and it will take a decade to repair them. But how long will it take us to repair the growing schism? Our children are growing up in a manipulated virtual reality. Every piece of media we consume has been doctored by some agenda. Social media is no different. This is not a new problem. It has simply grown exponentially, beginning with AM radio decades ago. We need to address our technical issues so we can go back to receiving bias-free news instead of tuning in to only what we want to hear. Teachers and thinkers have been saying this for a while now, but politicians are not listening. Politicians are not who the healing is going to come from: there is no savior in the wings; it really is up to us. We need to restructure a culture, a society that supports all genders and all bodies as possessing the wisdom to know what their gifts are, regardless of the roles society tells us are acceptable. This masculine-feminine polarity we live in is ridiculous; healing is part of the renaissance that is now being ushered in. It is not a short-term solution, but it is the only one I can see.

Trust. Speaking as someone who identifies as very feminine, I understand the challenge of remaining in your power *while* embracing vulnerability, especially when the old script for how women should think, act and feel demanded submission and compliance from many of us.

As we move forward into the future, how do we, as women and feminine folks, bring ourselves out of non-trust? I have become aware over the past several months that there is a deep distrust of intimate relationships that keeps my mojo down, distorts my intuition, and keeps me from the universal dance. The connection feels like an exposed wire. I know what I feel is valid, but boy has crazy been showing up! And I really do not like her at all. UGH! I am fine as long as I remain in my own orbit. But trying to merge in any way with others causes me to question so much. I don't even feel comfortable in my own skin! That is the distortion *for me*. The first step in creating trust is finding the distortion as it relates *to you*.

Before COVID, I was feeling so comfortable. I made huge shifts to create peace. Now we are all being forced to go in new or different directions. As I finish up this book, despite all my years of working on my distrust issues, I actually feel untethered. It has given me great pause because I want to come from a place of liberation, not trauma. As I have said before, this is not just about me. Everything we do now is not just for ourselves. It is for the collective, too. That is our responsibility. What we heal within ourselves, we heal for the whole. When we can hold a safe space for ourselves, everything can be fine. But my learning curve now is focused on how to hold my own wholeness and trust that I remain in wholeness while holding space with others, their experiences, and their wholeness? I am still dealing with trauma, but this feels much bigger because everything is not fine under the surface. The masculine and the feminine need each other; we need both energies within ourselves. The essence of trauma, regardless of where we are regarding our personal wounds, needs to be acknowledged for the sake of acknowledgment. Our job, *the* job, is to figure out how to trace this back to our own lineage, beyond our personal life experience. Some of this is generational, some of this is archetypal. It is part of our work nonetheless.

THAT IS THE FORMULA!!!

Instead of working all the time or being super independent, we need to find ways to follow through rather
than disconnect. We all have our own connections. Many
of my background and generation have had to forge their
own spiritual paths. Many of us forged our own paths
in the face of a lot of eye-rolling and other invalidating
experiences from our mates and others. So how do we form
relationships, get a real feel for what is going on? Where is
the essence of this? How do we form intimate relationships
after experiencing this type of divide? Man, woman, or
other, we have all experienced this deeply held pain of not
feeling good enough.

The modern challenge is this dynamic where the feminine
must *always* challenge the masculine. It will never be off the
table, and that sucks. But any woman who wants to create
change during this pivotal time must claim her power. On a
personal level, this can be exhausting. The sacred masculine
is that man who understands he is responsible for his own
shift. But let's face it—he is exhausted too. An equal playing
field is a new narrative. Sure, we have started, but in a way
that buys into the patriarchal ideology. For example, there
are patterns of transactional intimacy where we participate
in overly casual intimacy rather than true authentic connection and embodied intimacy. What are we, the feminine,
doing to be queens to our kings? We have to show up in our
own way. Whether that means owning land, having our own
money, or simply having full agency over our lives and bodies;
these concrete contributions actively challenge the societal

restrictions historically placed on the feminine. Remember, we have only been allowed to have our own bank accounts for half a century. It is very important to feel like we are enough, so the shadow of social weakness that continues to plague us *all* can be released. Ladies, feel your true worth. Find pride in your *own* ownership of self. And men, if you choose a true queen, remember she plays chess.

Both the masculine and the feminine have worked so hard to individuate that we have this fear of losing ourselves in a relationship. Men retreat mentally or just never open up, which stems from a lifetime of not being allowed to be vulnerable. Women retreat emotionally; we have been told we are too much or feel we have lost our voice, so we do not show our full selves in our true power. We need to restore healthy sacred sexual and emotional behaviors rooted in connection and intimacy. This is where the true restoration will take place. The masculine restores the masculine, and the feminine restores the feminine through the mentorship that my generation did not receive.

It is now time to restore mentorship. The Taínos have figured out how to harness it. It is collective within the tribe, which is also the family. Across cultures, similar customs remain. We must mentor through lineage: women to women and girls, men to men and boys, teaching the younger generations what we have learned about our shadows and legacies. We want to pass on the wisdom, not just the wounds. Then we can create social equity in all its required forms in our clans, tribes, and communities. Is it any wonder we are all feeling so tired, so distorted? The shaman is not only the medicine man; the shaman is the masculine and the feminine.

We have all lost our lineage or at least part of it. We need to facilitate the restoration; the distortions have become so obvious. Let's take a look at how the patriarchy has changed the meaning of sacred references toward women. "Witches" are feared when the original meaning was "wise one." When you hear the word, "hag" do you picture someone not put together to society's standards? It actually means "holy one." A few years ago, I was having a conversation where I mentioned stepping into our cronehood, embracing crystalized wisdom that comes with decades of experience. Boy, did I get a negative reaction from the women I said this to! A crone is not necessarily an elderly woman; it means "the crowned one." It is an obvious distortion, but we are still disentangling our enmeshment with these distortions.

I recently saw a social media post that asked, "Why is it we were taught to fear the witches instead of the men who were burning them?" Interesting distortion, and there are many more. I will leave that conversation to those who have more authority on these subjects.

Journal Questions:

1. What are your distortions? The first step in creating trust is finding the distortion as it relates *to you*.

2. We are leading ourselves back onto the path. The difference now, actually, *the question* now, is what your formula will be? How are you going to create a life that supports deep fundamental change allowing for new healthy growth?

"We do not believe in ourselves until someone reveals that deep inside us something is valuable, worth listening to, worthy of our trust, sacred to our touch. Once we believe in ourselves we can risk curiosity, wonder, spontaneous delight or any experience that reveals the human spirit."

E.E. Cummings

CHAPTER 9

Rituals and Practices from Peak to Every Day

Words don't teach, but they do tell. Giving us ideas for experiences. True learning comes through experience.

Drumming and rhythm. It has been proven that rhythmic sounds affect brain activity, recalling the sounds of heartbeats and footsteps. Therefore, the frequency of the drumbeat is important and universal. Different beats produce different brain states such as focus, memory, deep sleep, etc.

The theta wave state is one of the more elusive and extraordinary realms we can explore. It is also known as the twilight state, which we normally only experience fleetingly as we rise from the depths upon waking or when first drifting off to sleep. In theta, we can access information beyond our normal conscious awareness. This is why I always journal directly after waking up or coming out of meditation, writing down what is in my mind before it fades away. We are not yet making meaning; we are simply transcribing for the unconscious; we may not understand until later.

Theta has also been identified as the gateway to learning and memory. It is the state we achieve in deep meditation; it increases creativity, enhances learning, reduces stress, and awakens intuition and other extrasensory perception skills. When the brain is in theta, it appears to balance sodium/potassium ratios responsible for the transport of chemicals through brain cell membranes. This appears to play a role in rejuvenating the fatigued. It is where we go for deep restorative sleep, which is so essential to the healing process. The ideal drumbeat used is 4.5 beats per second. It is the third state after alpha and beta. If you want to know more, some experts have written comprehensive studies.

WHY JOURNEY WITH A DRUM?

Journeying is often, for me, accompanied by drumming. So I want to share the science behind the **why** of how it works. Let's begin by looking at vibrational frequencies: Nikola Tesla said that if you want to find the secret of the universe, you need to think in terms of energy, frequency, and vibration. Wouldn't it make sense that the energy and vibration we give off are met and reflected back to us through vibrational frequency?

We are all developing and evolving, tuning in to higher vibrations all the time. Do you notice that sometimes things just align? Ever tune in with a person or a situation and just feel like it matches your vibe? All our thoughts and emotions vibrate on a cellular level; each has its own energetic imprint. Drumming works because it allows the mind to slow and relax. It gives our brains an opportunity to focus on the tone of the drumbeat, stimulating a trance response. Drumming accompanies shamanic work because it raises your vibration to a higher frequency, thus allowing us to respond and take action in different ways. Albert Einstein said, "The problems that exist in the world today cannot be solved by the level of thinking that created them."[22] It has been my experience that shifting my mind with the drumbeat and allowing my imagination to journey will often give answers that come from a place completely outside the box.

Here are some drum beats you can use for a journey state.

I will use numbers for the drumbeats. The spaces in between are where you pause the drumbeat. You do not have to attempt to journey; you can simply create a beat that resonates with you.[33]

The Heartbeat

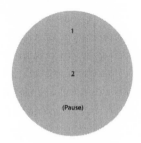

Living in the center of the drum is a way to merge your human heart with the middle world. It is a low tone and steady. 1, 2 pause, 1, 2 pause, 1, 2 pause. Just think of the sound of your own heartbeat. I often use this beat when I sing my medicine song.

The Go Away Beat—Clears Sacred Space

It has three steady beats. No spacing or skipping. The first beat is at the top of the drum. The second beat is at the bottom of the drum. The third beat is directly in the middle of the drum.

The Come to Me Beat—Draws in Healing/High Vibrational Energy

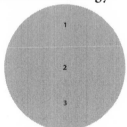

The first beat is at the top of the drum, with no spacing or skipping. The second beat is directly in the middle of the drum. The third beat is at the bottom of the drum

Horse Walk Beat—Facilitates Shamanic Journeying and Prayers

This beat is made by drumming 3-4 beats per second, rapidly in the center of the drum. But try to find a sweet spot: the place on the drum somewhere near the center where the tone is most rich. You can hear it as you beat. My small traveling drum's sweet spot is close to 7 o'clock.

Earth-Eagle Beat—Honors the Directions

This beat utilizes that sweet spot again, but this time four rapid succession beats, emphasizing the first beat. Emphasis in bold: **1,**2 3 4, **1,**2,3,4, **1,**2,3,4 **1,**2,3,4

The Ritual and Ceremony of the Shamanic Journey

STEPS FOR THE SHAMANIC JOURNEY
1. Opening Sacred Space
2. Breathing to attain an altered state
3. Drumming
4. Closing Sacred Space

STEP 1 OPENING SACRED SPACE

We can use our drum to open and close sacred spaces for ritual. Below is my own version of creating sacred space. You can create your own by grounding, listening, and working with the six directions. The element of water/emotion in the south, earth/body sits in the west, air/mind in the north, and fire/spirit in the east. The fifth direction is honoring our planet, the giver of life. The sixth is all that is, ether.

OPENING UNIVERSAL SACRED SPACE

I always begin in the south as I was taught to enter the medicine wheel and sweat lodge from that direction because it is how we enter into the womb before we embody life.

SOUTH–SPIRITUAL DNA–Law of Perpetual Transmutation of Energy:

This law states that, on an energetic level, everything in the universe is constantly evolving or fluctuating. Every action is preceded by a thought, with thoughts themselves having the power to eventually manifest in our physical reality. ***Changing the energetic frequencies of your thoughts changes your spiritual DNA.***

STEPS:

- Monitor your thoughts.
- Shift your thoughts with intention.

- Elevate the frequency by changing the negative through thoughts and actions.
- Shift your spiritual DNA to better align with the sacred.

WEST–MANIFESTATION–The Law of Vibration:

The Law of Vibration states that everything vibrates and nothing rests. Vibrations of the same frequency resonate with each other, so like attracts like energy. Everything is energy, including your thoughts. Constantly focusing on a particular thought or idea attracts its vibrational match. ***The Law of Attraction. Want love? Give love.***

STEPS:

- Focus on what you desire.
- Align with thoughts by taking action. Baby steps are fine.
- Believe in what you are seeking.
- Learn to vibrate at the level of your desires.
- Align with focus and belief to shift the vibration.

NORTH–HARMONY–The Law of Transmutation:

The Law of Transmutation states that energy moves in and out of physical form. Your thoughts are creative energy. The more you focus your thinking on what you desire, the more you harness your creative power to move that energy into results in your life. The Universe organizes itself according to your thoughts. ***Harmony is in everything that embodies the sacred.***

STEPS:
- Connect to what is sacred.
- Energy plus effort = attraction.
- Create the physical manifestations available to you.
- Sacred attraction creates.

EAST–HUMILITY AND LISTENING–Law of Relativity:

This law suggests that we are inclined to compare things in our world, but in reality, everything is neutral. Relativism exists in all things, and in the end, meaning comes down to our perspective and perception. ***Gratitude is key.***

STEPS:
- Listen with humility.
- Allow.
- Find gratitude.
- Shifting perspective creates gratitude.

CENTER–NATURE/THE EARTH–*Law of Rhythm:*

Cycles are a natural part of the universe. Physically, you can think about the seasons on earth. In our own lives, we can remember that integration is just as important as growth. ***Balance both productivity and rest.***

STEPS:
- Connect to your inner rhythms.
- Balance is sustainable.
- Ebb and flow.
- Allow for both integration and growth.

ABOVE–SPIRIT EQUALS LOVE–*Law of Divine Oneness:*

The first and most foundational law of the universe is the Law of Divine Oneness, which highlights the interconnectedness of all things. It says that beyond our senses, every thought, action, and event is in some way connected to anything and everything else. ***Thus, we are all connected through the web of life.***

STEPS

- Cultivate compassion for self.
- Cultivate compassion for others
- What would I love to do that allows for the divine law of compassion?
- We are Divine Love.[23]

STEP 2 BREATHING TO ATTAIN AN ALTERED STATE

Before beginning the journey, do this breathing exercise. There are several available. If you do yoga, you may want to choose one that you are familiar with. Though it takes concentration, it also takes you out of your monkey mind, helping you to embark upon an altered state of consciousness more easily.

THE 7:7:7 BREATH

Lie down on your back. Make sure you have everything you need. Use a drum or turn your body into your instrument. You can use your hands to tap soft beats on your abdomen, heart, or both.

Protect yourself. Wrap yourself in a cocoon or put yourself inside an egg energetically. Imagine light surrounding you. Remove any sticky energy that you feel and ask it to leave. Ask for only positive energy (high vibration) to surround you. Remember, everything is energy. Quantum physics tells us this. It is like electricity. It can be harmful or helpful. So it is important to only work with the helpful. Low vibration energies can be draining.

Begin by taking a deep breath in. Count to 7 as you are breathing in. You should be beating the drum (or tapping on your body) along with the counting. Hold your full breath to the count of 7. Again, beating to the 7-count. Slowly release the breath to a count of 7 while continuing to drum. Then hold your empty breath for the count of 7. The beat continues the entire time. Do this for 7 rounds. When completed, use the horse-walk beat for a spiritual journey. You can use the sample recording I created for my website: wildwomanishome.com.

STEP 3: DRUMMING AND THE JOURNEY

If you would like to record your own support track, read the below aloud and do so with several pauses to allow yourself time to breathe and explore. Speak or record as if lulling a child to sleep, slowly and with pauses that allow the drum beats to infiltrate your consciousness. Of course, you may also use the recordings available on my website.

The wonderful part of journeying is using the imagination to learn. Many newcomers to drumming circles would say, "I am not sure I journeyed. I feel like I was using my imagination." Then they would proceed to tell me about amazing experiences. My editor Viviana shared that most journeys she has experienced felt like little was happening, but upon reflection, there was more symbolism and imagery than the average dream would hold. I also happen to journey in black and white! I don't know why, but my journeys rarely happen in color. The key to learning to journey is to be open to the experience and to allow time to process. More insight will arrive into your understanding with time.

If at any point you feel uncomfortable or triggered by your journey and you need to stop, it is okay to take a break. You are not ruining the experience; you are exploring your own practice and boundaries. Just remember to go to Step 4 and close the sacred space for completion.

THE JOURNEY

When journeying, one goes into the upper, middle, and lower spiritual realms. If you are a beginner and drumming alone, I advise you to stay in the upper and middle realms. And always, before you begin to drum, imagine yourself in a protective egg or cocoon. Wrap yourself in a color that seems suitable or in white light, if that is your preference.

- Here is a short, simple journey. Unless you have this book on audible or are using the recording on my website, I invite you to record the following words beforehand in your own voice.

- (Use the horse walk drumbeat. We are going to the middle realm)

- Lie in a quiet, comfortable place where you will not be interrupted. Relax your body as much as possible. Imagine yourself in a favorite spot in nature, perhaps a meadow, a garden, or a beach.

- As you begin to drum or are listening to a drumming, look around with your mind's eye. Notice the light, how it touches the nature around you. Look for any trees or outcropping of rocks and just relax, enjoying this peace. Feel the warmth of the sun on your skin, the smell of fresh air. Usher in the feeling of safety and surrender.

- Now, with your body/mind, notice a softly flowing river off in the distance. Walk towards the river and take a sip of the cool, clear water, either dipping your hand in or putting your lips right to the surface. As you look up, notice there is a small boat for you to get into. Leisurely climb into the boat and allow it to gently take you on a quiet ride. As you move along, you are being cradled like a child, held within the boat. Your clothes are being lovingly stripped away by your ancestors or a trusted being. And without any effort, you are being draped in loose white clothing. Continue on in your boat, feeling dreamy. Just relax and feel the gentle movement. After a while, you will feel yourself come to a shore, to a gentle stop in the middle world. Now, as you take notice of your surroundings, you find yourself in a beautiful meadow. There is an outcropping of rocks in the middle; make your way there. Crawl up on the rocks. Sit quietly and begin to look around, feeling once again the warmth of the sun. Look at the surroundings of this magical place. Take note of what is there. Allow yourself to quietly observe. Are there trees? Are there animals present? Are there clouds floating? What else do you see? Is anyone there with you? Just spend some time in this place as you listen to the beat of the drum for a few minutes.

- (Few Minutes Elapse)
- In the far distance, you can see a castle. A horse is waiting to take you there. What color is the horse? What does it look like? You can communicate with this animal. What is its name? Its sex? How is it here to serve you?
- (Listen to the beat of the drum for a few more minutes.)
- As you climb onto the back of the horse, it will begin to move across an open field. Slowly, you will make your way to a castle with a moat surrounding it. Cross the moat via the drawbridge and enter through the open gate into the courtyard. It is bustling with people at the market buying their daily groceries. Enjoy the scene. Look around; do you see anything interesting? Continue to listen to the beat of the drum, then make your way towards the castle, up the stairs, through the massive doors

at the top of the stairs. As you enter, notice the beautiful tapestries upon the walls, the sweet, clean smell of the rushes covering the floor. Notice the feeling of this place of serenity.

- (Listen to the beat of the drum for a few more minutes.)

- Off to the side of the great room, you will see another stone staircase built into the wall. Go up the staircase. As you reach the top, you will find a small room filled with light and treasures. Look around the room, taking in the grand furniture, on top of which you may see all kinds of trinkets and baubles. Look up at what hangs from the ceilings. Observe the titles on the bookshelves. Is any gift, treasure, or book there for you?

- (Listen to the beat of the drum for a few minutes.)

- You can relax in this room; no one will disturb you here. As you explore, know that you are welcome to take any of the treasures offered; they are here for you. Don't worry; the horse will help you carry it back when you are ready.

- (Listen to the beat of the drum for a few more minutes.)

- Now it is time to make your way back. Allow yourself to move out of the room, down the stairs, and out of the castle. Find your horse, who has been waiting for you, ready to help you take your treasure with you. Notice if there is anyone who will travel back with you.

- Make your way outside the castle walls, back to the meadow. Dismount from the horse, saying your farewells to them and any other companions. Then make your way back to the outcropping of rocks. Crawl back upon them and take a look around. Are there any animals or people present around you? Make a mental note of what you see and hear. Relax for a moment on the outcropping, breathing in the fresh air, before heading back down to the shore where your small boat is waiting to take you up the river.
- (Listen to the beat of the drum for a few minutes.)
- Begin to make your way back to the boat, knowing and trusting that it will take you back to your original destination.
- (Listen to the beat of the drum for a minute.)
- You have been traveling upriver, receiving the comforting embrace of care from the boat once again. As you feel the boat gently land on the shore, go back to your favorite spot, where we started. Lie down and rest.
- (Listen to the beat of the drum for about twenty minutes. If you are drumming yourself, increase the drumbeat to a soft, quick drumming, several beats a minute. When it is time to return, the drumbeat should increase to a soft, quick drumming, several beats for a minute or so. This will bring you back into yourself and help ground you back into awareness.)

- Immediately after this journey, just rest and relax while your eyes remain closed. Take your time getting up. When you are ready, journal your experience. What was there for you? Were there any gifts or messages? Pay close attention to this. It is important to note that many, when learning how to journey, may fall asleep. That is just fine; your subconscious wanted the journey to itself.
- Keep practicing.

This altered form of consciousness is a wonderful tool to help you explore and connect. It is extraordinary, the connections that can manifest. Communication with guides and loved ones through this state can bring deep healing and even answers.

The above description of the journey mirrors one of my own. One time on a shamanic journey, I found myself in a castle with a small library. As I looked around, I could not see a gift. Then I lifted my gaze to see a teardrop pendulum sparkling in the light. A couple of days later, I walked into a little crystal shop, and there it was! Sitting pretty in a case was a good size crystal for a pendulum, like what you would see on a chandelier. But there was a dark smokey area in the quartz crystal identical to what I saw in my journey (dream state). I still have this piece and cherish it. This kind of thing is not an isolated event. Altered states bring the unconscious to consciousness. It brings gifts into the mundane.

There is also a lot of literature available if you'd like to go deeper in your exploration of altered states. In the last decade, there has even been a resurgence of spiritual podcasts that you might want to explore.

ADDITIONAL PRACTICES

Grounding, a momentary meditation.

Even if it is only to step outside in your yard to put your bare feet on the earth to ground, do it. Grounding has been scientifically proven to change the cellular makeup of the entire body. It is believed that all sorts of inflammation and pain are associated with our lack of connection to the earth. This is a real thing! We no longer wear shoes made of leather that allow for the energy of the earth to reach the soles of our feet. Since we live and grow and depend entirely upon this earth, does it not make sense to stand on her to start your day? Or even to end your day. As I mentioned earlier my favorite grounding practice comes from the Toltec. Each day I begin by standing with my arms raised to the heavens and say, "**With all my love and no fear, I greet this day.**"

Indoor Grounding–
Grounding through the forward fold straddle.

This exercise was introduced to me during a kundalini yoga class. As I was in this pose, I thought *Perfect way for those that cannot step outside to get grounded*.

1. Begin in a downward-facing dog. Make sure your inner elbows are facing each other, and your hands

are flat. Focus on your index finger and thumb, making sure they are firmly planted on the mat.

2. Bring your feet up on the outside of the yoga mat in a straddle position, a wide-legged kind of half-lift, activating your glutes. But keep your ears aligned with your arms.

3. Now begin to go up onto the balls of your feet, then down to flat feet.

4. As you are doing this, begin to focus on the breath, breathing in through the nose and out through the mouth. Make the "ha" sound on the out-breath: this releases toxic buildup. Doing this with a drumbeat is optimal.

5. Try doing the above for five minutes. It really helps with grounding while getting rid of the muck. Stop if it becomes too tiring. Slow down before stopping.

6. Then go into an easy pose, sitting cross-legged on the mat.

If you are still not feeling grounded after sitting for a moment, you can simply move into a half-staff pose. Sitting with your feet straight out in front and toes pointing up, bring your hands down to each side of your hips. Lift yourself up off the ground. Then gently drop. Do this a couple of times to move the energy.

Drop cords through the root energy center down into the earth. Wrap them around the earth's core.

And remember, if this all feels too much, then dance. Dancing and shaking your body up are always good ways to get grounded. Plus, it makes you happy!

Make an intuition notebook.

We begin by becoming a mirror. This means nothing more than reporting everything you are sensing, feeling, and thinking, but you do it out loud. Record yourself, be natural. To do this, begin when you are relaxed. Take some deep breaths.

1. Take a deep breath into your abdomen. Expand it as you breathe in. Hold it. As you breathe out, release that air out of your abdomen up into your heart and your higher or upper heart (chest area). Do this several times. Breath back in from the upper heart back into the abdomen.

2. Report and record every experience, thought, memory, and feeling.

3. After recording, write it down. Do not write from your conscious mind and only write on paper, no typing. It is ok if it does not make sense. Do not edit your words to appease the judgments of your conscious mind. Stop writing or recording after a few minutes. When it feels natural, take a break. Finally, if you feel stuck, take a deep breath.

For me, this is where I find it very important to tap into my body's wisdom. It never lies. The difficulty is that we need discernment to interpret our findings well. Is it an old story? Is there something in our past or even in an unconscious past that we are not aware of? Is this something implanting a fear? Or is this real, justifiable fear? If you are in doubt, treat it as real. But remember, you really do not know. So move gently in your decision-making process, especially if others could be affected.

Yoga or Stretching

The most important facet of my yoga experience and what I teach has to do with the connection between our sacral region and our heart. Every day I focus predominantly on these areas. It has taught me mindfulness with the body. While loosening up the entire body is important, I always allow for opening in my thighs, hips, and heart. At the end of every yoga session, whether it be in my personal practice or while taking or teaching a class, the final pose is typically one that targets the sixth and seventh energy centers but works with all of them because it allows for a deep rest that balances the digestive, nervous, and endocrine systems as well as the entire body. While it cultivates relaxation at the end of the movement, it is also very beneficial when you are feeling anxious or stressed, and it can aid in lowering your blood pressure. What works best for me is meditation after an hour or more of yoga to interpret and integrate what may have been released in my tissues. This final Shavasana, also known as dead man's pose, symbolizes not death but freedom through spiritual awakening.

SHAVASANA

Below are the instructions given at the end of all yoga classes. This, too, can be recorded.

1. Begin by lying flat on your back; knees bent toward the ceiling, feet on the floor. Your feet and knees should be aligned with the hips.

2. Take your hands into a T, off to each side, palms down. Turn your head to the left then to the right. Tuck your chin toward your chest then relax your

head and neck. Now lift your tailbone slightly, tucking it under thus allowing your lower back to connect to the mat as well. Slide your feet forward, extending the legs straight and allowing the toes to drop open in opposite directions.

3. Roll your palms so they are facing up, and slide your arms closer to your body, at about 45 degrees.

4. Notice any tension, and then relax your body, bringing your awareness to your feet. Look for anywhere you are holding tension as you travel your awareness up toward your stomach and abdominal region. Make sure you focus on the lower back as you release the tension from the abdomen and glutes.

5. Let your heart area relax, releasing any thoughts of breathing. Let the middle back relax. As you release the tension from your chest, rest your upper back, feeling your shoulders melt into the mat. Let your throat muscles go; release the neck and head, making sure you unclench your jaw. Soften every fiber of your being, including your internal organs.

6. Close your eyes. Rest peacefully for three to five minutes, then bring your awareness back into your body. Softly begin to wiggle your fingers and toes. Personally, I do not like the wiggling, so I do not do it, but some folks really like the way it feels. Instead, I skip this part, or maybe I rock my head, first toward one side, then the other.

7. Now, gently sweep your hands along the ground, bringing them together above your head. Stretch

your feet out long, as you bring them together as well. Like it is the first stretch of the day as you are lying in bed, bring your knees and feet up, so the feet are flat on the ground, knees shining up. From this position, roll onto the right side of your body (if it is early in the day) or onto the left side (if it is later in the day), pillowing your head with your arm.Take the free arm and place your palm on the floor, elbow bent.

8.   Rest in this fetal position for a moment, then when you are ready, slowly roll up to a seated position.

If movement is not something you can incorporate into your daily routine, then listening to a beloved story while lying in this pose is an amazing way to release anxious energy. If you struggle with depression or have been sexually traumatized, try doing this pose with your knees bent toward the sky or ceiling, feet resting wider than your hips, and your knees closed. You may also try this just for brief periods until you feel more comfortable. And instead of having your eyes closed, it is just fine to have them softly open.

Remember Your body–your comfort–your healing! There is no right way, only what feels right for you.

Yoga notes: One of the reasons I like yoga so much is because it is accessible: it offers us movements that we can do. Personally, there are so many moves and postures that I can't do. But I have fun trying and visualizing and enjoying the growth that the practice will offer me for the rest of my life. The challenge of going from a modified pose to a non-modified pose brings joy. Yoga allows for a rich spiritual experience as well. Or not. It's up to you. For some, just being able to be in the body with the practice of breathing through movement is enough. For others, there are breakthrough practices that heal. Yoga poses work to open the energy centers of the body, as we discussed in Chapter 6. Our connection to nature can be expressed through this practice. Remember what you read regarding the energy centers? It really is remarkable. But yoga has a mindful side to explore as it is closely linked to meditation. It is a good place to start if you want to bring mindfulness into your daily life.

MINDFUL MEDITATION

If you are new to meditation, understand that you will likely never experience pure clarity of mind in how we think it should work. Rather, our goal is to be present in our bodies, with our minds, noticing the sensations and thoughts entering our space. That can be challenging to start with, so I recommend meditating directly after yoga or movement practice. Yoga, in its origins, was developed by the gurus to tire out the students so they could learn to sit for meditation.

To try this, I invite you to take a seated position cross-legged on the floor with your knees lower than your pelvic bones. I like to sit on a block, blanket, or pillows to elevate the pelvis. This allows for a longer and more comfortable sit as you meditate. If the floor does not work for you, take a straight-backed chair, feet firmly planted on the floor. Once seated, turn your palms upward to receive, or simply lay your hands wherever feels comfortable for you. You can also lie on your back with your hands and feet uncrossed.

1. Focus. When your focus wanders, bring it back. This is why many use the universal sound of "aum," pronounced and written in the west as "om."

2. Working with the breath, inhale O and exhale M.

Meditation is a state that allows for "new" to come into your inner being. When we pray, we typically ask for a blessing. When we meditate, we ask *What is it I can do for spirit?*, allowing the quiet to settle in. It is remarkable the messages one can receive simply sitting quietly.

For beginners, I suggest mindful meditation practices. You can use the phrase *I am at peace* as a beginning mantra. Inhale "I am," exhale "at peace."

Mindfulness allows you to simply observe where your mind wanders. Pay attention to where the thoughts go and gently bring yourself back to your mantra. Please try not to become frustrated with your wandering mind; we are simply noticing where it goes, without judgment. As with the journey work, these are practices. They are called practices for a reason! Ask any professional athlete how much practice they have put into their craft, and you will likely hear that they are always training.

If meditation is too difficult, then simply focus on positive thoughts and positive interactions you have had with others. Simply relax and go into a state of appreciation.

"All that you are seeking is also seeking you. If you lie still, sit still, it will find you. It has been waiting for you a long time." Clarissa Pinkola Estes

Claiming personal sovereignty can only be accomplished from within. Your essence has the answers. By doing short meditations once or twice a day, you can harness moments of intelligence, deep calm, and contentment.

Finding a source that provides guided imagery is even better as it works with all the physical systems and thus the symptoms of stress we spoke of in earlier chapters. I recommend this, especially if shamanic drumming is not your cup of tea. Check out Biogenics under additional resources.

Self-help books are great. Hell, I just wrote one! The barrage of baggage that flies at us can feel overwhelming and triggering at times, and yet we strive to find ways to continually heal and evolve ourselves. What I have written in this final section are tools for you to use, simply carved down to bare bones; you may incorporate your personal practices and other touches that feel right to you. It doesn't all have to be done at once—sometimes, I find myself stepping away from deep spiritual work to spend some time just living life! You may choose one or even all of them to practice if they will help with the emotional experience of living in these challenging times.

Another mindfulness practice can be simply learning to communicate with nature through sensory experience. We begin with the understanding that we are a part of all that is. What do you see around you? What do you hear? Do you feel any tactile sensations? Do you notice any smells or tastes tickling your senses? We step into our personal power through surrender. We surrender by deeply tuning in and listening, releasing the ego. Also, by releasing the old paradigms of thinking that believe we hold dominance on this planet. We do not. The planet holds the dominance; COVID is teaching us that. The earth will continue long after we are gone; it is important to tune in to her teachings, embarking on new understandings that will help us on a personal level but also enhance life on earth for us as a species. Nature is original intelligence, and it is the guardian of all life. Those who are original thinkers, i.e., indigenous cultures, believe that social healing will happen through dialogue and believe it will happen collectively rather than individually through mutual aid and collective storytelling. Narrative healing is very important because it is a way to let the Spirit speak through stories. Thought is vibration and is tantamount to the intelligence of nature. This book has a similar approach to *You Are the Universe*[24] in how it covers western thought and the erroneous belief that our thoughts are separate from, or even superior to, the rest of creation.

For more information, you can also check out the Circle for Original Thinking, "an inclusive, grass-roots think tank. Our mission is to seek out the deep origins of contemporary thought in order to remember and restore heart-centered wisdom for humanity and all our relations on Earth. We accomplish our mission through intercultural dialogue circles, ceremonies, workshops, and conferences in partnership with like-minded organizations. We invite your participation and support. Membership is open to all."[25] Now, more than ever, we have to find ways of marrying our streams of knowledge.

The above exercises are uplifting and important for our balance and well-being. But the best part, and I do mean the very best part, of all of this is to achieve a deep connection to nature. This is really the essence of wild woman work. Once we accept that all of nature, even rocks, have a spirit, we can begin to communicate. For me, this is the most easily done with cats, dogs, and horses. There is deep learning that can come from these domesticated animals, as well as other animals. Have you ever thought to yourself, *Maybe I should take this course of action* and then see a hawk or owl fly directly over you? This is the spirit of nature speaking!

By simply sitting and listening, we can telepathically communicate with anything. Whales, dolphins, turtles, deer, bears, and eagles, as well as rocks, crystals, plants, and the stars. The possibilities are endless. This is why I have introduced shamanic drumming in this book. Sitting quietly and drumming is a wonderful way to meet and get to know your spirit guides and allies, with the purity of heart and simplicity of mind.

The Law of Attraction and Manifestation: Is it all it's cracked up to be?

"The secret is the answer to all that has been, all that is, all that will ever be."

-*Ralph Waldo Emerson*

I was first introduced to this concept in 2006, around the same time I began my graduate program and was learning astrology. I deeply regret not paying more attention to how empowering working with vibrational energy is. There are those who will roll their eyes here but bear with me.

Part of the wild woman process is to face fear and release it into self-love. This includes the fear (which is a lie) that we are not good enough. Once we learn we are good enough, then there is a new fear: the fear of how big and wonderful we really are! Pay attention to your thoughts around fear because the moment you think, *Well, that's not possible,* then it *is* no longer possible. You are the source and the creator of every moment of your life. What do you want? It is really very simple; it is the same thing that we all want. Sadhguru says (and I am paraphrasing), *We want wellness and pleasure in our bodies, our minds peace and joy, emotionally we want love and compassion, energetically we want bliss and joy.* It really is that simple!

Fantasizing about exciting life experiences, choosing the delicious possibilities, knowing and being *grateful for the coming adventures* we dream of are the first steps in bringing about the change we want. Begin by being thrilled when you get those passionate thoughts and feelings; this leaves you wide open to manifest what you desire. There are many videos and books on this subject offering digestible thoughts and concepts that teach you how to allow what you desire to come to you. It is just a matter of looking at what you do not want in your life, thanking it for showing you this contrast, then shifting your focus and intention on what you do want.

An Energetic Exercise

Harnessing ways to work with our well-being energetically is so important because, as many are coming to understand, we are not just physical bodies. Science is finally catching up to this. Our subtle bodies, the etheric, emotional, mental, astral, the casual, and even our auras can all be recognized as pathways to healing. It is why energy healing works. Motion is important in the context of energy flow. Trauma or Inherited Cellular Memory can cause blocks in our systems. Any energetic movement is medicine; there is so much out there to explore—so make it an adventure! You are the expert in your experience and will become the expert on your own healing. Trust in your essence; it never lies.

Try this one exercise to prove it to yourself:

Find a comfortable seated position. Extend your hands straight out in front of you, palms down. Make a fist, then release. Do this 20 times with both hands.

Then, flip your hands over and make the fists again 20 times with both hands palms up. Then, face your palms toward each other about six inches apart. There are several energy centers in your hands, so you should feel the energy moving between your hands.

Repeat the process. This time, when you are done with making the fists, rub your hands together and put them over your heart space.

I do not remember where or who I learned this from, but it has been a favorite of mine.

To conclude, I want you to know that you are loved and supported in this healing journey you are on. May you find yourself closer and closer to your authentic self.

Love,
Patricia

ADDITIONAL RESOURCES

BIOGENICS–a course I have been doing for several months. I use it as an addition to everything because guided imagery and sound waves are used to train the brain's neuroplasticity, the neural network. To put it simply, it works by remapping. There is so much more to be said about this subject. But for now, just think of it as a way to retrain your brain. This course "is a tool for reducing stress, anxiety and pain. It is a skill to help you when you need support–it trains you to be stronger–it helps when you feel hurt–it strengthens your character."[1] Plus it is easy to do and very relaxing.

Introduction to Emotional Freedom Technique (EFT/Tapping)Courtesy of: Susan Harney, LMFT, EFT Practitioner/Trainer

Susan offers teacher training to those who would like to offer this modality to others. She can be reached at susan-harney@rocketmail.com

Tapping is a technique that has grown in popularity exponentially since Gary Craig launched this modality in 1995. This is a tool I believe everyone should have in their skillset, and all psychotherapists should be trained in. Tapping works on the energy system and is under the umbrella of what is called Energy Psychology. I first learned about Energy Psychology in early 2007 while attending a Bruce Lipton & Gregg Braden conference in southern California. I was so excited about it I immediately started studying Gary Craig's videos for my own healing and to help others. For me, Energy Psychology is the missing link in psychotherapy. Talk therapy is important and has its place in the healing process; however, trauma and painful stuck emotions need to be removed at the energy level as well. Tapping does a wonderful job and works quickly at doing this.

Not only does tapping greatly accelerate the healing process of trauma and traumatic memories, but it also helps to remove challenging emotions in the moment and can be used anywhere! Additionally, this is a technique most anyone can learn to use, so you don't need the help of a professional indefinitely.

So how does it work? Gary Craig, I believe, gives us the best answer, and that is to think of it as *psychological acupuncture*. We have energy lines in the body called meridians, and these meridians are connected to various organs in the body. Gary found that certain acupoints in these meridian lines can also store challenging emotions. When tapping on specific acupoints, the energy body releases these emotions and brings the body into balance. This often occurs within minutes. Research has shown tapping over time actually changes neural pathways and works directly on the amygdala (our flight, fight, freeze, fawn response).

It also changes brain chemistry by releasing endorphins. Furthermore, because the emotional body and the physical body are connected, as you heal the emotional body, the physical body heals and vice versa.

There are many videos that teach people how to tap, and it is simple to learn. However, there is also an art to it. The better you get at tapping, the better your results. When tapping, you want to be as specific as possible. For example, to tap on the emotion "anxiety" is very general. You want to identify what is causing the anxiety. For example, maybe you have a test coming up, so you would tap on "anxiety about my upcoming driver's test." If you can get to the root cause of the emotion or the belief that is creating the emotion, that's even better. This is where a professional can really help out. Although you will feel the effects (generally more peacefulness) of just tapping on a general emotion, lasting results come from being more specific and getting to the root of the issue.

People frequently ask, "How often should I tap?" and I say as often as you think about tapping. You cannot hurt yourself by tapping too much. The more you tap, the more sensitive your energy body becomes and the quicker it brings the energy body to balance. Tapping throughout the day is especially helpful with chronic anxiety. Oftentimes people have no idea what is causing the generalized anxiety, so just tapping as often as possible on this anxiety will help relieve it. Another benefit of tapping and releasing intense emotions is increased clarity on the problem. This can allow you to tap more specifically on the issue, so eventually, you won't be triggered by it. An experienced practitioner can really help you get started with clearing deeper issues, and then you can use the tool as needed.

There is so much more that can be learned about EFT/ Tapping that isn't meant to be covered here; however, I hope you will explore this tool further with either an EFT Practitioner or YouTube videos. EFT is a revolutionary tool that has changed my life and the lives of so many; you owe it to yourself to do some research and see if it is a tool that just might change yours! Much love to you on your journey. May you find the peace and well-being that is waiting for you…. Namaste, Susan

Acknowledgments

A special acknowledgment to my editor Viviana Scarlet Niebylski, MA, I cannot begin to convey my thanks and appreciation. She is a shining example of a human being: patient, kind, brilliant. Her contributions were many and varied. She opened my eyes, improved upon my words and concepts, made me back them up with facts, and frankly made it a much better piece of writing.

Thank you to Melinda Joy Polet for the consultations. You helped me immensely through the creative process.

Thankful appreciation to Charlene Springer for the wild woman photographs. You're a maestro.

Rosi Lusardi, thank you for painting my medicine wheel drum. It's holding up beautifully.

Endnotes

1. Clarissa Pinkola Éstes, "Women Who Run with Wolves: Myths and Stories of the Wild Women Archetype," in Women Who Run with Wolves: Myths and Stories of the Wild Women Archetype (New York: Ballantine Books, 1995), 157.

2. Christopher Parry, "The Shadow," January 4, 2018, https://www.thesap.org.uk/resources/articles-on-jungian-psychology-2/about-analysis-and-therapy/the-shadow.

3. PBS, "Basics of Buddhism," accessed April 7, 2020, https://www.pbs.org/edens/thailand/buddhism.htm#:~:text=In%20Buddhism%2C%20desire%20and%20ignorance,them%20can%20only%20bring%20suffering.

4. Echart Tolle, A New Earth: Awakening to Your Life's Purpose (New York: Penguin, 2005) 14.

5. Mary Carroll Nelson and Don Miguel Ruiz, "Beyond Fear A Toltec Guide to Freedom and Joy: The Teachings of Don Miguel Ruiz," in Beyond Fear A Toltec Guide to Freedom and Joy: The Teachings of Don Miguel Ruiz (Tulsa: Chicago Review Press, 2020), 51.

6. Margaret Crastinopol. Micro-Trauma: A psychoanalytic understanding of cumulative psychic injury. New York: Rutledge, 2015.

7. Dr. Joan Rosenberg, "Emotional Mastery: The Gifted Wisdom of Unpleasant Feelings," TEDxSantaBarbara, September 21, 2016, YouTube video, 15:17, https://www.youtube.com/watch?v=EKyl9WzkPxE.

8. Maria-Barbara Watson-Franke, "A World in Which Women Move Freely without Fear of Men: An Anthropological Perspective on Rape," Women's Studies International Forum 25, no. 6 (November 2002): 599-606, https://doi.org/10.1016/S0277-5395(02)00338-2.

9. "Prayer for the Earth: An Indigenous Response to These Times," Films For Action, accessed March 25, 2021, https://www.filmsforaction.org/watch/prayer-for-the-earth-an-indigenous-response-to-these-times/.

10. Stan Rushworth, "The Changing Earth: Indigenous Voices from Turtle Island," accessed July 27, 2021, https://www.thechangingearth.net.

11. John L. Payne, The Healing of Individuals, Families & Nations: Transgenerational Healing & Family Constellations Book 1, (Scotland: Findhorn Press, 23.

12. Carlos Castaneda, The Active Side of Infinity (London: Thorsons, 1999).

13. Phil Borges, "CRAZYWISE," CRAZYWISE, December 11, 2018, https://crazywisefilm.com/.

14. Lisa Miller, "Depression and Spiritual Awakening — Two Sides of One Door," TEDxTeachersCollege, July 24, 2014, YouTube video, 15:52, https://www.youtube.com/watch?v=7c5t6FkvUG0.

15. Phil Borges, "Psychosis or Spiritual Awakening: Phil Borges at TEDxUMKC," TEDx Talks, February 23, 2014, YouTube video, 25:02, https://www.youtube.com/watch?v=CFtsHf1lVI4.

16. "Isabel Allende Hopes Pandemic Will Doom 'Patriarchy,'" Global Times, June 8, 2020, https://www.globaltimes.cn/content/1190916.shtml.

17. Stephens, Mark. (2012) Yoga Sequencing, Designing Transformative Yoga Classes, North Atlantic Books. Berkeley, California , USA(p. 295)

18. Katie Kiss, Cecelia Burgman, and Darren Dick, "Native Title Report 2008 Chapter 6: Indigenous Peoples and Water," Australian Human Rights Commission, accessed on September 19th, 2019. https://www.humanrights.gov.au/sites/default/files/content/social_justice/nt_report/ntreport08/pdf/chap6.pdf.

19. U. S. Geological Survey, "The Water in You: Water and the Human Body," accessed 10/13/2019, https://www.usgs.gov/special-topic/water-science-school/science/water-you-water-and-human-body?qt-science_center_objects=0#qt-science_center_objects.

20. Wallace J. Nichols, Blue Mind: The Surprising Science That Shows How Being Near, In, On, or Under Water Can Make You Happier, Healthier, More Connected, and Better at What You Do (New York: Little, Brown and Company, 2014), 16-17.

21 Dr. Tony Phillips, "The Worsening Cosmic Ray Situation," Spaceweather.com, July 10, 2018, https://tinyurl.com/6yv2cm6t

22 TBU News, "Pineal Gland - Solar Storms and Human Biological Effects," TBU NEWS , August 9, 2017, https://tbunews.com/pineal-gland-solar-storms-and-human-biological-effects.

23 To learn more about how we are all connected check out: Everything is Connected -- Here's How: | Tom Chi | TEDxTaipei https://www.youtube.com/watch?v=rPh3c8Sa37M

24 Samantha Schmidt, "No Game Days. No Bars. The Pandemic Is Forcing Some Men to Realize They Need Deeper Friendships.," The Washington Post (WP Company, December 4, 2020), https://www.washingtonpost.com/road-to-recovery/2020/11/30/male-bonding-covid/.

25 Anya Silverman, "The Ancient Crone," Crones Counsel, accessed March 25, 2021, https://www.cronescounsel.org/the-ancient-crone/.

26 Robert Lawrence Friedman, "The Healing Power of the Drum," Remo, accessed March 25, 2021, https://remo.com/experience/post/the-healing-power-of-the-drum/.

27 Mateusz Konopacki and Guy Madison, "EEG Responses to Shamanic Drumming. Does the Suggestion of Trance State Moderate the Strength of Frequency Components?," Journal of Sleep And Sleep Disorder Research (2018): 16-25, https://doi.org/10.14302/issn.2574-4518.jsdr-17-1794.

28 "Brain Wave States," Brain Wave States, accessed March 25, 2021, http://www.metempyrion.org/brainwave_states.html#.

29 https://www.mindbodygreen.com/articles/the-12-universal-laws-and-how-to-practice-them

30 Deepak Chopra and Minas C. Kafatos, You Are the Universe: Discovering Your Cosmic Self and Why It Matters (Rider, 2018).

31 "Circle for Original Thinking," Original Thinking, April 6, 2020, https://originalthinking.us/circle/.

32 https://www.biogenicscourse.com/sales-page-477800231617916875248

33 Author Unknown; All One Tribe drum; Access date unknown: www.allonetribdrum.com

Made in the USA
Middletown, DE
18 July 2023

34847558R00099